Thousand
Acre
Marsh

A Span of Remembrance

Thousand Acre Marsh

by DUDLEY CAMMETT LUNT

THE MACMILLAN COMPANY
NEW YORK 1959

First Printing

The Macmillan Company, New York
Brett-Macmillan Ltd., Galt, Ontario

Printed in the United States of America

Library of Congress catalog card number: 59-10295

For
N. W. P.
Who has been predicting this book
for a generation

Contents

Foreword

I once had a friend whose ambition in life was to acquire experiences worth owning. His argument was that they constitute the only real wealth in this world. An experience that is really worth having and owning, he would point out, does not have to be insured. It is never subject to any tax, and your executor will never have to account for it. And your heirs will relish their recollection of your tale of it. As a matter of fact, he used to say, such an experience was about the only thing a man could acquire that someone else did not have some kind of a stake in. Such experiences are really your own—to have and to hold for keeps. A man can relive them in his mind all his life.

I have found his advice to be good.

The experiences in this span of remembrance have been gathered out of a lifetime. Their locale is in the place of my origin—along the coast and in the woods of the State of Maine—and in the rolling hill country and the eye-stretching coastal plain of the place of my adoption—the State of Delaware. Indeed in their common location and descent out of the settlement of the Atlantic coastline, to the discerning eye, each has much that is common to the other.

DUDLEY CAMMETT LUNT

The Spring
of the Year

A distinctive aspect of any shore line lies in the character of its marshes. They differ widely. In New England they line the shores of a thousand and one little salt rivers, lying flat and yellow between the fir-crowned spurs and ridges that rise on either hand. Spanned with ribands of blue when the tide is in, when the tide is out they are the source of the succulent clam and the habitat of great flocks of shore birds.

Contrast this with North Carolina where, separated from the pounding ocean by a thin ridge of sand, a wide bay of brackish water lies bordered by acre after acre of marsh covered with tall wavering fronds. Here no man may walk, nor is there tide save as this body of water is shunted to and fro by the prevailing wind and alternate calm. Here is the winter home of the last of the swans—white, tall, and stately. Here also is the caravanserai of the wildly discordant Canada goose and of myriads of wild duck swift flying on whispering wings. Here the striped bass abound in a vast profusion.

On the shore of the Delaware River, we have it both ways —the tidal and the fresh-water marsh. If you follow the river road from New Castle through Delaware City, you will see what I mean. After crossing the bridge over the Chesapeake and Delaware Canal you run out on a causeway. On the river side of the road lies the tidal marsh, and here, as anyone who has ever gunned it will testify, is a rugged day's work. The viscous mud is more than knee deep and with a receding tide the water pours off this marsh, sweeping out of the guts into the river as if poured from a gigantic pitcher.

The shore side of the causeway on your right hand is in sharp contrast. Here the water is shallow and it is fresh. As your eye carries across to the rising farm land beyond, it stops here and there, arrested by a muskrat house or the occasional gunner's blind. For the gunner this fresh water—this Thousand Acre Marsh—is a deal pleasanter; though when a howling northwest wind slants the snow down the cut, here too it is a rugged job to get out into your blind, rig out your tollers, and then get safely home again with a couple of brace of sprig, teal, or black duck.

This is no natural phenomenon, this split marsh. It is man made and it dates, some say, from the days when the causeway was a dyke erected by the early Dutch settlers in these parts. In the memorable Thanksgiving storm of 1950 great breaches were washed in it. I was glad when the repairs got under way and I applaud the fact that a unique and distinctive feature of the Delaware landscape has been restored.

In the spring of the year you may with profit to your soul lazy away a whole afternoon on the shore of Thousand Acre Marsh. Pick yourself a dry log at the water's edge and stretch out your weary legs. Let the afternoon sun warm you up and make your miserable life more comfortable. The gentle breeze from off the river will bring to your nostrils for sniffing that penetrating and peculiar smell of the marsh. A curious compound of the luxuriance of the new growth mingling with the rich decomposing of that of the last and all the yesteryears, it is akin to a first breath of salt air off the ocean.

This breeze brings you still more—for your ears a chorus of the strangest calls, clucks, chuckles, cackles, peeps, whistles, quacks, and trills you ever have heard, for the marsh teems with bird life. And for your eyes there is further feasting—a vast expanse of green millet weaving gently with the breeze, broken here and there by the brown rounding dome of a muskrat house and the clump of dead grass that masks and marks the gunner's blind. Away in the distance where the tide gate lets St. Georges Creek through to the river, blobs of red, yellow, and blue bespeak the sport shirts of fishermen.

Wheu wheu wheu—then again *wheu wheu wheu*. The shrill whistling cry of the winter yellowleg. I call in return. He echoes in reply. There he is, wings set, swinging in a long tangential arc toward the shallow water beyond the first tussock of grass. He wheels. The glide flattens. The long slender yellow legs droop. Then of a sudden he is down and feeding busily with his long sharp bill thrust deep down into the mud.

With a sweep of the glasses I follow frequent flights in twos and threes of the wing-flashing blue-winged teal, and now a dozen and more leap out of a cove to the right, to wing out over the marsh and plash, still flying it seems, into a far-away pool. My eye is caught by the sight atop a muskrat house. There stands and struts a mallard drake. Now and again he whips his wings with powerful strokes, throwing out his chest. On top of another is a night heron in a solemn and silent stance. I see three geese outlined against a dark pool. Then one of them beats its powerful wings. The duck are in constant flight across in front of me, first rising, then scaling on poised wings toward some distant pool. Once down they are soon lost among the tussocks.

In the calm air of a spring evening the calls of all this wild life are impressive. The mallard, busy at their nesting, are constantly quacking, and from away off on the marsh, hidden by the tall fronds of the feather grass, the wild geese are in the midst of a gabbling talking converse. Over all is the frequent soft *gurgulee* of the red-wing blackbird I see here and there balancing on a wavering stalk. Through all this medley there comes softly, now and again, that strange and familiar note—the booming of the bittern, or stake-driver as he is so often called—a curious belching, welching, watery sound.

In the spring of the year I often spend an afternoon and early evening here by the side of Thousand Acre Marsh, watching its teeming life and listening to its symphony of wild notes.

Do you know what, in old Delaware parlance, a cripple is? No! Well, the meaning is remote indeed from the usual connotation. I once encountered this cripple in the reading of an ancient statute enacted over a century and a third ago, which incorporated the Black Bird Creek Marsh Company. By its terms a dam was authorized to be constructed by those who lived alongside and owned the "marsh, *cripple*, and low grounds bordering Black Bird Creek." Then a turn of the leaves of Webster informed me that this archaic localism connoted swampy or low wet ground, often covered with brush or thickets.

Down along the Delaware River and Bay a legion of little salt creeks and rivers wind in tortuous curves through vistas of eye-stretching marsh. Here it is that you will find the cripples. When the salt creeks commence to narrow, long tongues of land stretch beside them. Wet underfoot these cripples are and thick with tangled underbrush, and, where I was this afternoon, supporting a sturdy growth of white oak. It is curious how sharply the upland is marked off from the marsh. A man will plant his corn right to the very edge of it. Thus I can step from solid terra firma, or fast land as they call it, into the thick black muck of the marsh. Then as the little creek winds around his cornfield the farmer will perhaps leave this shore, this cripple, to wild growth. Here is a haven and a heaven for birds. The trees form roosts for the wild doves—silent graceful forms silhouetted against the sky— who alternate between their perches there and their arrow-straight flights out over the fields to alight and feed. As I pass through into the thicket I flush any quantity of small birds. Come evening in the fall of the year, the ducks and geese follow these watercourses as guides to the remoter cornfields of the peninsula. Here also in the fall are coveys of quail that later scatter before the gunners' approach.

A sudden sharp call, unfamiliar and hence compelling, rivets my attention to the scarlet head of a bird against the gray trunk of a maple. Thus for the first time I see the red-headed woodpecker. This always is an event. Then comes a scuttering through the leaves underfoot and the flashing in zigzag flight of a cottontail. Also I carry back with me the remembrance of long wavering filaments of gossamer, glancing and gleaming in the slanting path of light cast by the setting sun across a brown and green field. And this sight too, like that of the woodpecker, is one of first impression.

What a place to be in the spring of the year when all that rich earth is bursting with green life and the birds are at the height of their singing.

I live at the edge of Bringhurst Woods. Here a small two-storied cottage of gray field stone faces the southern quarter.

Flanking the door on either hand thick clumps of rhododendrons rise in rounding curves of green to the height of the eaves. A climbing rose clusters around a pilaster of the porch. To the right a maple towers aloft giving an abundance of welcome shade. Beyond on the lawn there is an Atlas cedar, a wide spreading pin oak, a ginkgo in angular display, a line of dogwoods and then a hedge that is the border of an orchard. To the left beyond a flower garden there stretches an open field.

Always when I emerge from the house I see the birds I have flushed in ascending tangents of flight out into the woods.

To the west where an ell houses the kitchen, there rises a white oak. I remember it as a sprout. Rising by the back door to shade the well is a dogwood that is a perfection of proportion. There is a woodshed and in the woods a small cabin. To the east there shoulders high into the sky, stretching its long limbs and wide branches far out over the sloping roof, a great beech. Hard by in gaunt outline rises a Norway spruce.

Enclasping the cottage as in a crescent there range around the back and the two sides the towering trees of Bringhurst Woods. In the depths of these woods is a spring. It overflows into a brook. In turn this empties into Turkey Run. And at length the Run conjoins with Shellpot Creek. All this courses between the ridges that form its watershed. There is a cave; there are cliffs. And over all there tower the tall trees that weave with the winds—a great variety of deciduous growth —oak, maple, poplar, beech, dogwood—and the evergreens —white pine and hemlock.

This is an isolated environment. It is a proper spot for the concentration of migrating birds, a place of wild flowers, and the habitat of a variety of small animals—gray squirrels that frisk in the trees, a tortoise observed in a ponderous traverse of the lawn, rabbits that scutter in the beam of the headlights when I drive in at night, opossum, racoons, fox, deer, and many another mysterious creature that is heard and unseen.

With the spring the robin, who is ordinarily a somewhat solitary fellow or to be seen in pairs, suddenly becomes gregarious. When I emerge suddenly from the house they burst out of the rhododendrons in clouds. The other day in the shank of the winter I counted fifteen who had chosen a temporary headquarters in a tall maple. It was in the late afternoon and the falling light threw them into sharp relief against the bare branches. With a good pair of field glasses I could make out their claws clasped around the twigs, and the effulgent color of their breasts sharpened by the refraction of the glass. At such a time when the daylight is slowly fading, binoculars are truly rose-colored glasses.

But wait! Caught in a perfect focus one of them leaps into flight. Without spreading his wings he launches his body and that graceful downcurve is for all the world like that of a diver in a swan dive. The glasses follow him down. With a burst of his wings he slips into the depths of a tall holly. For a moment he is lost, and in seeking him out, the glasses range over the holly—a depth of deep green leaves with the rich red of the berries gleaming in clear outline against them.

Of a sudden he stands in focus again, stalwart and upright, his chest aglow against the deep impenetrable greenery of the holly. With his beak agape he clasps a single red berry. Then with a sudden toss of the head it disappears down his throat. He ducks, plucks another, and then stands there with the berry a spot of gleaming red in his bill.

Here in the framed field of my binoculars is an Audubon print come suddenly alive.

A couple of days later when I again visited this holly, it

was utterly bereft of berries. The robins had stripped it.

This morning with my first glance out the window from my bed, my eye glimpsed a familiar figure. Perched upright on the bare gray twig of the beech that grows by the corner of the house was a small gray bird, just a bit bigger than a sparrow. Now and again his tail gave a quick twitch. Then came the soft, clear and unmistakable call—*phee-bee*. From this familiar couplet of softly sung syllables the phoebe derives his name.

Year in and year out now I have seen this bird on this perch of his in the beech. From there it is but a short step of a flight —perhaps fifteen feet—to where the old gray, mud-encrusted nest lies on top of a wooden cornice under the eave of the ell. Here, this year, still another brood is destined to be reared. Throughout the spring I will see him or his mate perched on this beech twig. From time to time he will shuttle forth in a short circular flight. I will hear the little metallic snap of his bill as he catches some luckless insect, and watch him return to his perch and then fly up under the eave where a deal of noisy fluttering will betoken the feeding of a wide-open maw. And the still, soft, spring air will now and again resound with his *phee-bee, phee-bee*.

A little later this fellow will be joined by a competitor, another small flycatcher who takes his stance out in the woods nearby on an outer branch of a dogwood. He will sit quietly, there will be no twitching of the tail in the sojourns between his circular forays after the elusive fly. But now and again the soft air will resound with his lazily whistled call—*pee-wee, pee-ur-wee*.

This is the wood peewee.

The most exciting events in Bringhurst Woods take place

after nightfall. I recall one cool spring evening when there sounded outside and near the house, a sudden sharp snort. Then came a pause and then another snort and still another. This could be nothing but a deer and a buck at that. Darker than the inside of a dog, it was, and hence just the night for jacking deer. And so in a trice I was swinging from outside the back door a broad beam of white light, stabbing the darkness and casting the undergrowth and the trunks of the oaks into shadowed outline. Slowly the beam swung, searching at the height of a man for a pair of gleaming eyes. Then came that noise again—sharper, close at hand, and to the right. I swung the beam dropping it, and it came to rest at the foot of a huge hemlock.

It was no deer. Close to the ground there shone two close-set yellow eyes. The mouth opened and the cry rang out, still sharp and clear but with a harsh gutteral quality. Unmistakably it was a snarl from jaws well armed with small sharp teeth. It was not a fox for there was no brush—nor a racoon for there were no rings. And it could not be a mink. It was too large. Slowly the creature began to back away uphill in the beam of the flashlight. Above those yellow agate eyes, the small ears rose to a point. . . .

At this point in the telling of the tale, my listener—a seasoned woodsman who dwells on the shore of the Penobscot River in the State of Maine—suddenly reached forth his hand and touched my knee:

"Most pro'bly," said he, " 'twas a bobcat!"

Indeed it is only occasionally that one is aware of the eyes that watch unseen in the night. On another night the cool stillness was shattered by the abrupt clatter of a tin cover on the stones bespeaking a raid on the garbage bucket. Again the beam of the flashlight sweeping around the brush at the back of the house soon picked them up. A pair of eyes agleam in the blackness, swinging, blinking, and backing away in the beam. What was it—dog, skunk, coon, opossum, fox—what? The gun was still in the rack. I never knew.

These are the rare times when yours are the unseen eyes. But consider how often the reverse is the case and you are the one who is watched. The suburban and farm land of modern Delaware is a superb terrain for small game. And certain it is that this wealth of game sees you far more often than you glimpse any of them. There is solace in this for the timid and the lonely. For they may reflect that at night in the country-side they are never alone. A myriad unseen eyes are watching them.

Every now and again the Norway spruce, that stands tall and tapering with its top hamper dry and dead, hard by the corner of the house, has a nocturnal visitor. Of this there is proof in the morning. The scaly bark of the limbs and trunk and the brown leaf mold beneath the wide-spreading branches are discolored by splashings of white lime. Also, scattered here and there on the ground are little rolled-up gobbets of fur and small bones—the regurgitated remains of a luckless field mouse swept aloft from its lair by a pair of clutching claws. Then I know that we have had a visit from *Strix varia*.

But more often he makes his presence known from a distance. And I know of no night sound more enthralling, more compelling, than the hooting of this hooting owl. You *have* to listen to him. From afar his hooting echoes through the aisles of the woods, a soft melodious rolling *whoo whoo* deeply yet subtly tinged with melancholy. But the sound is quite different when he is close at hand in one of the dead upper limbs of the Norway spruce.

The other night, a cold one, when I was snugging close to the hearth, I heard one, though the windows were shut and the blinds closed. A muffled sound, hardly more than a mere throb, it seemed. Yet the second set of hoots fetched me upright, and directly I went and stood at the open door. A clear, cold, dark, blue night it was with the pale moon on the wane and giving but little light.

Then his call came sharp and clear. Each note was a distinct throb, and this close—I could not have been fifty feet from the bird—the first of each double *whoo* seemed to end shut with a *t* at the end. Like this:

hoot whoo.

They were clearly defined, each hoot being a separate syllable. In a series of two they came forth in the still air, four of them:

hoot whoo.

Then a pause, and again:

hoot whoo.

Another pause, perhaps the merest dite longer; and again:

hoot whoo.

And then the final concluding:

hoot whoough.

It is this sequence of four double calls that gives rise to his nickname—the Eight Hooter.

I never saw him that night. I just listened. In fact, I did not go out for fear that I might startle him off his perch and thus put an end to his unearthly concert. *Strix varia* is a shy creature. Yet I have seen him in Bringhurst Woods. I recall once at dusk as I walked past a thick holly, and he loomed out of it on a vast wing spread to scale silently off into the darkness.

Why did this lone owl sit there and send forth in a regular succession his eerie calls? With what partner did he converse? Why all this rolling melancholy, ringing and throbbing through the night air? The hooting owl has his reasons, no doubt. But I know them not, and that is a part of his melodious and mysterious appeal.

Hoot whoo—repeated thrice and then the signing off—*hoot whoough.*

When the dead end of winter is behind you, that is the time to get a good head start on spring. And the best way to do this is to practice the uncomplicated art of forcing. This nurturing of the wild spring blossoms indoors is simplicity itself. When you are out on a walk take your jackknife along, or slip a pair of clippers in your pocket. Who knows what you will bring home to put in that empty brown crock over there in the corner after you have filled it with clear cold water—pussy willows perhaps with their promise of golden fuzz, or for your table a blossoming clump of green-leafed snowdrops, the brown stems of forsythia destined soon for the glory of yellow, or if you are lucky, a few horse-chestnut branches. These latter will make you a conversation piece for weeks as their buds slowly burst and their leaves emerge. They take on at first the form of tiny cupped hands and then stretch forth their fingers toward the light.

This year I struck it rich. Up back in Bringhurst Woods I came upon a clearing where someone had been cutting up a red oak log for next winter's wood. On either side the brush had been cleared, and there strewn about was a goodly supply of wild azalea, by some known as the pinkster flower. I cut a few tops, set them in water, and waited.

For quite a bit—this forcing calls for patience—there was nothing to indicate life save the slowly swelling buds. Indeed there was nothing to distinguish these branches from dead brush. Then one morning there commenced a small unfolding of pale green at the tip of the buds. Daily it grew, the green paling, then merging with and finally yielding in a closed blossom to a most delicate shade of pink. Then came the surprise of surprises. Those close-clasped clumps of pink suddenly shot forth a group of slender stalks and the petals of the pink buds unfolded in a white so intense as to reduce their pink to a pale mauve.

Thus finally the spreading brown branches utterly bare of leaves were crowned at their tips with cluster after cluster of flowers, and this glorious spectacle filled a south window with all the charm of a flower print.

Out of season the duck hunter has his occasional vicarious thrills. Tall tales they tell, those who have gunned the Arkansas flats, of the flights that flash through the branches of the trees and drop with sudden splashes in the swamp. Well, one April day I had a rare taste of this.

I was on the way to work, early in the morning with the sun well down below the skyline of the trees. Passing over the bridge there they were in Shellpot Creek, a pair of mallard. Tossing on top of the white water, the green head and deep purple speculum in the wing of the drake shone with iridescent splendor. In a dark pool below a large rock the hen swam unconcerned. Suddenly they were startled. Heads cocked and tilted sharply. There was an alarmed quack and then, with that familiar leap aloft high into the air, the pair of them were mounting toward the treetops. As they swung with the course of the creek, this duck hunter's arms came up in simulated aim. Mark one on the drake and then in my imagination the hen tumbled too. A nice double. But by this time the two of them were flashing from sight amid the leaves.

This stirred a lot of memories and put me in a good humor for the whole day.

I have a friend who in the fall of the year at the full of the moon and when it is high in the sky will sit and watch it through a pair of powerful field glasses. For answer one night, when I put the inevitable question, he passed over his binoculars. The valleys and mountains stood forth in sharpened outline in the clear cold light. Then of a sudden high in the air there swept in silent flight across the face of the moon a flock of migrating duck. In a trice the wide V had come and—had gone. The sight was etched in my memory. I gasped. No word was spoken. My friend just reached for his glasses.

At the end of the day, too, the flight of waterfowl is a memorable occasion. Once from a crowded city street I glanced aloft to glimpse for that moment a single duck winging rapidly toward the eastern sky. Against the pink afterglow he was in sight as he emerged from behind one roof top to be eclipsed by another, but the length of the glance. Yet his dark swift passage left an indelible impression.

At Chincoteague, after the geese have rested all day long on the foreshore, they will string out in wavering black lines that stretch from skyline to skyline against a pink-tinted mackerel sky. In Currituck Sound after the day in the blind is over and the boat is running you home toward a hot supper, you will watch and watch with ceaseless fascination as now a flight of geese clambers aloft out of the path of the boat, again pitches far ahead, or wings across your course, the air resonant with their tumultuous clangor as their powerful wings beat with majestical precision. These are rare moments for later remembrance.

One evening at dusk near the head of one of the nameless

creeks that floods twice a day and then pours its accumulated waters back into the Delaware River, I was witness to a remarkable evening flight. Before sundown it commenced as now a single and now a double flashed up the course of the creek. Then came the broken calling, telling of geese in flight, and a long line—fifty at least in a single file—flew in over the peninsula and then out of sight and out of earshot. Now the ducks were flying—small flights that came in seemingly from nowhere were in sight for a bit and then disappeared out over the fields. The massed flights came after the sun had passed the skyline, fretting the naked limbs of the trees in a pattern of black lines.

Finally there came the flight of flights—hundreds upon hundreds of ducks. A loud, a noticeably loud swish of wings was the first evidence of their presence. I glanced aloft. Overhead the air was black with ducks, wings set, scaling down into the small marsh. Then they were low, flying in tiers, wheeling and circling. The soft *kuta-kuta-kut* of the feeding call betrayed them to be black duck. Doubles and triples broke off and flew counter to the flight, making a weaving pattern against the paling sky. Then they swung out over the cornfield beyond the far side of the narrow marsh, and for a moment I saw them there through the bare limbs of the trees in a flight that was equal to the height of those trees.

Then of a sudden, as suddenly as they had come, they were gone. The air which a moment before had been filled with ducks was now clear of them. It was as if I had been witness to an apparition. And the sight of them through the trees just before they settled in the corn has remained in my mind with the sharp clarity of an etching.

In aid of these remembrances I keep a cache of feathers, and as I write I turn in the sunlight between my left thumb and forefinger a small one, just three inches long. It is tipped with white and one side of the shaft is gray. As it turns and the sunlight strikes the other side at a different angle, a deep blue turns into a brilliant green. Let these feathers be multiplied and lie, one overlapping the other, and they bespeak the swift zooming flight over the top of the feather grass of the little green-winged teal.

Next I take up a larger feather—it measures four and a half inches long—and watch a dull olive-green sheen as it becomes, with a slow twisting, flecked with strands of bronze. This is from the speculum of the sprig or pintail. Next in my collection is a beautifully curved specimen, even longer and also tipped with brilliant white that runs into black and then merges, as I twist the stem, with a deep shade of purple shot throughout with the merest suggestion of red. This is of the familiar mallard drake whose gleaming green head is also iridescent. Then there is that of the black duck—a cunningly commingled dark purple and blue.

And so at last I come to the prize of the collection, a single feather from the wing of the drake summer or wood duck whose entire plumage in season is a glowing mass of iridescence. Of him the manual says, "Male in Winter and Spring Plumage: Highly iridescent, descriptive words fail." But do they?

Slowly I turn this tapering feather. At the trailing edge the predominant color is red, a dull yet shining crimson. This merges with a burnished gold streaked with green. Then toward the tip a now purple, now blue, and now green sheen shines with my turning. And this is but one of how many thousand feathers that go to make up the brilliant plumage of this magnificent bird.

Those who complain of a late spring—wet, dark, dank and endlessly raining, may take solace in a few of the records picked at random from random sources since the Reverend Johann Campanius first kept track of the daily weather in these parts in the years 1644 and 1645. In the spring of the year 1765 there occurs on the 24th of March in the Field Notes of Messrs. Mason and Dixon, a laconic entry—"at 9 in the morning the snow was three feet deep." Then on three successive days they bracketed their terse record—"Snow so deep we could not proceed."

Consider what would have been the state of your garden in 1816 when in every month of that year there was a frost, and snow fell in the summertime. And just over a hundred years ago, as is revealed in a familiar lithograph, just below us here at Havre de Grace, the old Philadelphia, Wilmington and Baltimore Railroad, in the winter of 1852, laid its tracks on the ice across the Susquehanna over which in a six weeks' period there were trundled ten thousand tons of freight.

Coming a little closer to home, Hodgkins, who resurveyed the Twelve Mile Circle in the nineties, reported that he was forced to suspend work in late March because "The winter weather was of almost unprecedented severity for that latitude, the temperature for many days at no time rising above the freezing point and falling 35 degrees or 40 degrees F. below freezing at night."

Now I submit that an April that is wet and chilly is a blessing in disguise. For in such a season spring comes forward slowly, almost with circumspection. I can watch it come in and savor its growth. I have the pleasure of seeing the trees in Bringhurst Woods feather out before their leaves unfold. Indeed a late spring is much to be preferred to those bursts of unseasonable heat that bring on summer weather and the foliage to the fullness of its blooming, almost over a weekend.

Take the dogwood. The first thing I notice are the buds. They begin to swell a bit. When I trim a branch that has trespassed on the driveway, the sap wells forth and a drop falls from the severed butt. In those days punctuated by wind and spells of rain, the buds go on swelling. Then here and there one opens slightly and the folds seem to give promise of a green blossom until there comes a morning with a hot sun overhead. The petals begin to emerge and the green edges are seen to border on white. There follows a day or two's cold spell, and this nascent flowering is caught in a state of suspended animation. Then comes a really warm day that quickly unfolds the four-petaled blossoms to the fullness of their bloom.

If this coincides, as it sometimes does, with a full moon, I can enjoy the privilege of a walk at midnight to observe the towering patches of white blossoms that are gleaming here and gleaming there in the depths of the woods. Ghostly and pale they are trees set apart by their whiteness and the pale light. They have a spell cast upon them, these dogwoods in the moonlight, and the sight of them casts a spell upon me.

On these early April mornings when the woods and trees are just beginning to feather out, when the air is damp and the shrubbery still drips from the early morning's shower, a winter visitor to these parts makes known his presence by his singing. This is the white-throated sparrow, a chunky brown little bird that I often see hopping in leisurely fashion from branch to branch in the depths of the thick rhododendrons, hardly distinguishable by the faint streaks of black and white on his head and that white patch on his throat. It is the call that comes from his white patched throat that makes his short sojourn here in the spring of the year so memorable an occasion. His call is easily imitated—a slow and clear piping whistle that seems first to rise and then fall away to a soft note in a minor key that is thrice repeated.

They are plentiful hereabout and once after an early spring thundershower I counted fifty of them feeding in a leisurely traverse of the lawn. They talk to one another, these white-throats, as the morning rain is clearing and when I stand in the depths of Bringhurst Woods, which are alive with them, I can participate in an animated conversation. Downeast folk call him the Peabody bird.—*Pea-pea-peabody, peabody, pea-body*, they say. And some will say that the call resembles: *all-day fiddlin', fiddlin', fiddlin'.* Here today and gone to-morrow is the whitethroat en route to his summer home in the valleys of the rivers in the north of Maine, where in the deep quiet of the deep woods his clear piping call gives one on a hot summer morning a dimly religious feeling.

On the 28th of July in the year 1857 Henry Thoreau was in camp on the shore of Chamberlain Lake and he recorded:

"When we awoke we found a heavy dew on our blankets. I lay awake very early, and listened to the clear shrill *ah-tette-tette-te,* of the white-throated sparrow, repeated at short intervals, for half an hour, as if it could not enough express its happiness. Whether my companions heard it or not, I know not, but it was a kind of matins to me, and the event of that forenoon."

No sight is more characteristic of the Delaware countryside than the flight of blackbirds. With the approach of dusk any day now there comes to ear from afar a faint chorus of *tchirps* and *tchucks*. I look aloft and there in the sky, far above the trees, they are—myriads of little black bodies, each one flow-ing, as it were, in a short zooming burst of flight—the en-semble a great caravan of the air. It is an exciting event and it stirs the blood, this streaming of endless flight across the sky.

In late afternoon as I pass an abandoned farm—a cellar hole, a tottering wall, a tangle of unkempt brush, and a clump of maples—a flock flies in. The maples are to be their roost for the night. Directly an uproar assaults my ears. Their chatter is incessant, almost deafening. Then I notice one thing. Perched in the tops of the maples, each and every blackbird faces in exactly the same direction. And so motionless do they stand, it is like a great set piece, as if the conical tops of the trees had suddenly matured a growth of black fruit. Occasionally the illusion is shattered as a single blackbird flutters out of one tree to alight in another.

The deafening din continues. It is almost irritating in its persistence. I decide to try a trick that never fails to propel a blue heron into flight. Cupping my hands I bring them together with a *clop-clop.* Instantly the chattering ceases as completely as when a tap is suddenly shut off tight. Every blackbird is in flight and *in the same direction,* which explains what I had noticed of their stance. Now the great cloud of small black bodies is sweeping in a wide symmetrical curve back into the tops of the maples. There never was a military maneuver of such precision as this flight of the blackbirds. And with their alighting their sociable gabble begins again.

This happened on the way to the mailbox. A fluttering by the roadside caught first my ear and then my eye. A small bird it was, thrashing its wings in the thick grass. It rose a few inches and fluttered in effectual flight perhaps a couple of feet, then came to rest crouching close to the ground. Was it injured? I stepped toward it.

Then followed a chase into a tangle of scrub pine, the bird

fluttering into flight just as I would reach over to pick it up, and shrewdly leading me to where the growth was thickest. At length I caught it. Then when I opened my cupped hands for a close look, it burst up into my face. The chase was on again.

What was it? The feathers were an indistinct gray-brown and it seemed to have no distinctive marking. A sharp tail and pink feet with delicate claws. Suddenly it stood in profile and the erect stance was unmistakable—it was that of a pigeon. And then I knew it to be a young mourning dove. Again I caught it and calmed its struggles by stroking the back of its head until it crouched in my hand with its dark, liquid, beady eyes alert and alive.

I secured it under a screen in a wooden bucket in the dining room. My hope was that it would commence to coo. These mild mornings in May I often hear doves in flight as their wings go whistling by and then from afar in some tall tree or from an erect perch on the telephone wire there comes the soft muted call—*coo-coo-coo.*

The next day I took the bucket outside and lifted the screen. Instantly the young dove leapt aloft and mounted in strong flight to an upper limb of the Norway spruce. There it perched for perhaps a quarter hour. Then it left in swift flight for parts unknown.

Probably all that had been needed was the accrual of its strength.

I sit on a huge log on the east bank of the Brandywine. It is a peaceful spot. The ripples of the rip out in front are dappled with the light of the slanting rays of the setting sun. The incessant slap and gurgle of the rushing stream and the soft susurrus rustling through the emerging foliage absorb and mute the sounds of mankind in the distance—a low rumble of heavy timbers as a car passes over the covered bridge hidden above the bend upstream and the recurrent snarl of a distant power saw. Now and again from a thicket on the other side of the stream comes the lisping, lilting song of a song sparrow.

As the curving course of the Brandywine runs twisting, now around a tree-crowned knoll, and then in the opposed turn of the S, past the shoulder of a timbered ridge, it leaves first upon the one hand, then upon the other, a broad level meadow. The log on which I sit lies on a high bank at the edge of one of these meadows. Its flat floor stretches in broad expanse from the tree-lined bank on to the foot of the wooded ridge that causes the next turn in the stream downstream.

This meadow on this May day is the mead of the poets. Here Persephone must have danced at dawn. Its verdure is spotted with buttercups that incline their golden faces toward the setting sun. Violets grow underfoot in thick purple clusters. Here and there considerable stretches of blue-white show where the bluets grow in close company. As I walk in the shadow of the trees lining the bank I come upon clusters where the pink and the blue of the bluebell give to this mead a luminous aspect. In one low and shady spot the pink is so pale as to suggest the anomaly of a white bluebell. Underfoot in a thick carpet of green stems are masses of little purple flowers that are unknown to me.

In the trees that border this meadow there is a constant silent flitting of birds. Now and again a blackbird wings in zooming bursts of flight across the open expanse to alight in the upper branches of a single sycamore that stands in the middle of the meadow. For quite a spell I watch the unconcerned flittings of a pair of myrtle warblers. Then a creaking tells me without my looking that a mallard is passing in evening flight. A few moments later, where a vista through the trees opens up a stretch of the stream, I see a pair of them floating on the surface. There are red-wing blackbirds, their burnished red-gold epaulets gleaming as they turn toward the sun. As the afternoon dies I watch high in the newly feathering leaves of a tall red oak the repeated forays of a pair of crested flycatchers.

When I leave, the shadows have stretched across the meadow to the ridge on its farther side. But the trees on the side of this ridge are still bathed in sunlight. The delicate differences in the pastel shades of the different kinds of growth and the slight chill in the air faintly suggest the fall of the year. It is evening in the valley but still daylight in the hills.

At the turn of the road, there they were, the pair of them. Youngsters—straw hatted, sport shirted, and blue jeaned— they were plodding up the side of the road toward the railroad tracks, carrying their short bamboo rods pointed carefully ahead. Red and silver spinners splashed glancing rays from their rods as they walked.

I had to drive on. It was time to get to the office. Yet this short encounter sustained me all day long. Midmorning I caught myself wondering where they were and how they were making out. Were they beating their way up the hidden course of some obscure brook? Were their creels filling up with shining beauties? Did they know of some hidden pond far from the highway? Or perhaps they were dozing in the warm sun upon some high bank.

At noontime I sought out a fisherman friend to take to lunch and thus wet my line in good company. And all the day long there came to me from time to time in the swift flash of a mental close-up—the backsnap, the twirl of the line, then the cast and that lovely round dimple where my fly kissed the water. Not that I soldiered on the job. Not a bit of it. Never did I do better work or feel the better for it, all on account of that chance encounter that morning with two young fishermen.

The experience put me in mind of the rituals of the spring of each year. There are those who say that the green pea marks the peak of this season, and I once knew one whose ambition it was to start in Florida and come north with the green pea, arriving, as it arrived, in each locality along the way. A worthy ambition this, but it would take a man all spring and all summer and into the early fall. For I well remember one cool evening in early September in camp on the shore of the upper St. John River having a tin pail filled to the brim with fresh green peas and boiled to a succulent turn.

Now with the shad it is different. Come the late winter, they assemble at some hidden rendezvous out there on the continental shelf beneath the wide Atlantic. There they pick out a stream that drains the seaboard, at the head of which there lurks a likely spot for their annual amours, or perhaps, as some now claim, they simply head for the sandy bed of their own spawning. Then they are to be seen leaping upstream, and as the spring advances the markets of the waterfront resound with familiar cries—the Carolina shad, the Potomac, the Chesapeake, the Susquehanna, the Delaware, the Hudson, the Connecticut, and so on down east until at last and always on Memorial Day they run up the Nonesuch on the western coast of Maine. And always along each stream, they are the very best shad in the world.

Come the spring of the year in Delaware, the proper time for shad is just as the trees are beginning to feather out. For a prime result you want a fire in the open, preferably of white oak or dried-out dogwood, if you can get it, burned down until naught remains but a bed of coals alive with little blue flames that, leaping aloft, will sear first the skin side and then the flesh. But first grease your broiler and grease your fish, and then there will be no adherence to the grids of the broiler. Turn her often, turn her frequent—there is the secret. For then the juices run down back through the flesh with each of your turnings of that broiler over the glowing coals.

And when the magical moment comes—that perfect moment—pull her off the coals, slide her onto the hot platter, garnish her with the green of fresh water cress, with the yellow of sliced lemon, the light brown of dry bacon, and the darker brown of the hot roe. And then just as quick as you can, eat her, while the juices are still turning to aroma—the whole washed down with a Pouilly Fuissé of the best vintage chilled to just the proper pitch.

The experience is akin in remembrance with the devouring of a square-tail a generation ago. In the north of Maine the square-tail is the common brook trout. In the early days they grew there to fabulous proportions, and nowadays you never hear of the brook trout—only of a little square-tail, or better still, a big square-tail trout.

"They was so thick there in them days, in that pocket by the dam at Sordy-hunk," I have heard an old-timer recount, "that a man couldn't sleep nights what with them big square-tails o' their'n a-slappin' the water all night jest like rifle shots."

Sordy-hunk is still well known to the angler, though perhaps more familiarly in its properly spelled form—Nesewad-nehunk Lake—and its proper pronunciation which is achieved by sounding the letter *n* in advance of the word "sword," and then winding up with "nahunk," like this—Ner-sword-nahunk.

It was on a warming sun-drenched day in June, long ago and well remembered, when I, a tyro, was at the butt end of a long rod there. We were trolling. The canoe, a great flat-bottomed twenty-footer, was skimming through the cat's-paws, touching the waters lightly, steadily propelled by long, slow sweeps of the Frenchman's paddle. We had been at it for quite a while. It came to be past our nooning, and this was a hungry Frenchman who sat there in the stern.

So he made me a proposition. And directly we swapped roles, I taking the paddle and he the rod. His first step was to dispense with what he called "that gesely gilpoke o' yourn" —a very fancy shining spinner that had been most highly recommended by the well starched clerk where I had out-fitted. Then a second or so later I watched a slab of white bacon go drifting astern just below the surface. There was a short direction or two—to keep the pace steady, to leave the fishing to him. Then we were as we had been before—two men, the skimming canoe, the broad level of blue water, the shores ascending in unbroken forest to the skyline and there to the east'ard the towering massif of Ktaadn.

I watched the Frenchman. A little man, lithe and lightning quick he was, clad in a black jersey that seemed more hole than jersey. Beneath the brim of a tall-domed black hat, affected by all lumbermen and river drivers, which he kept cocked at an atrocious angle, his eyes were slanted upward toward the tip of the rod. Squatting on the bottom with his legs crossed akimbo, as one might say, he was the epitome of the quizzical.

Of a sudden the rod snaps. The reel crackles. Tensed, the Frenchman sits alert, now giving line, now reeling in. I stop paddling to watch, and astern the water breaks and there is a sudden arch of beauty. His yell sets me to paddling again. Steady, steady, keep her steady. The line whips and saws, this way, that way. The rod bends, an alluring curve. Now the hand net is overside. There is a sudden jerk aloft, and there enmeshed in the twine is the encircling curve of a big square-tail, glistening, dripping.

"How you like de *poisson* I ketch fer you, aih?"

Suspended from a thumb thrust between the gills the Frenchman holds the square-tail up for inspection. A shining glistening beauty of mottled coloration it is, and immediately there ensues speculation as to its size. This is settled upon an ascending scale of credulity that runs like this:

"If a man say, dat feesh, he weigh two an' a half poun'," opines the expert, "dat man, he crazy."

So the bid is raised to three pounds. The black hat is re-cocked and a further appraisal is made:

"Well now, I tink as how she weigh more as dat."

And so now it goes to three and a half. No response. Four? is queried softly. A flash of white lightens the sallow countenance in the shadow of the black brim. The four and a half brings the murmured response:

"Well mebbe now, we stretch dat square-tail, jes' leetle mite, aih?"

Then:

"What we hangin' round here for?"

The bow of the canoe swings and we head for the shore. Already the expert's eye has picked out the lunch ground, as always, a regular home. There is a slight grating as the bow bites into the sand. Then the black hat and tattered jersey are quickly lost to sight in the brush, and from the direction of their disappearance there comes the steady *chunk chunk* of an axe. This is followed by a smothered crashing sound, and a few seconds later the butt end of "a ol' pine stub" comes looming through the bushes to be thrown down with a thump.

The Frenchman starts at one end of the log. With the second blow a huge chip spins out. Then the axe flashes over his head in a back-handed swing that bites into the butt right at the back of the wedge already cut. The stick falls off. The Frenchman moves along the log. There is a repeat performance. At the end of the log there is no respite. He returns splitting each stick into quarters as he goes. And again there is no stopping, for again he back-tracks, picking up the split wood as he comes. At the end of the now split-up log, he kneels, quickly constructs an open crib of the split sticks, pulls a curl of birch-bark from his hip pocket, strikes a match, and the black smoke begins to curl up through the crib. Then as the following flames crackle, he speaks his first word:

"Where's dat square-tail?"

Out of the empty firkin it comes. Rapidly is it gutted, head, tail and fins cut, and then split. Now in a propped-up broiler, with his back to the small breeze off the lake, he faces it to the flames, and thus it is broiled in the open by the shore of Lake Nesewadnehunk—Sordy-hunk as some call it.

Now there is a little time for ease, for contemplation, for appraisal, for enjoyment. Now and again the Frenchman turns the broiler to the flames, and the firm pink flesh begins to sear here and there with lines of black.

Ah, the remembered taste of that square-tail.

I like crows. Every morning as regular as a clock the

caucus that lives in Bringhurst Woods wakes me up. I hear them agoing it out in the tall limbs of the oaks in back of the house. Their cawing is incessant and every now and again it rises to a crescendo as they burst out of their roost like black sticks blown aloft by a distant explosion and busy themselves in circling flight, cawing all the while. What is afoot? No man can tell, but there is much ado about something. Perhaps they will alight again, perhaps not, and in the latter case they are off for some unseen destination. Then I will listen for their cacaphony coming in from their distant rendezvous.

Every day or so I make a trip out into the woods. This is one of the small chores and the purpose is to dump for future burial a box full of accumulated bottles and tin cans. Always I can count on the rising flight of two flapping black forms that ascend without warning *caws*, missing the branches of the trees yet never swerving. Never, no matter how carefully I go, do I come upon them on the ground. Always they are in rising flight.

I recall now, once upon a long time ago, being in camp alongside the Grand Falls of the St. John River in a grove of tapering spruce. By chance this was a crow roost, and equally by chance the crows did not roost there that night until after we had turned in and all was quiet. The next morning both campground and roosting place lay buried deep in a thick gray fog. When I stepped outside the tent I could not see the tops of the spruces. But a crow saw me.

Then commenced an unforgettable show. In the thick fog the crow, ordinarily a most sagacious creature, became confused. Great black-winged forms came flapping toward me through the mist, wheeling, scaling and circling through the spruces—terrified at the sight of man, yet more terrified by the loss of familiar bearings. Their incessant cawing carried a special note of terror and despair at being thus lost, for they dared not leave their roost for the vast unknown. At long last the sun burned through and released them. Then, as suddenly as it had commenced, the show was over. And as we put our canoe into the stream, the last crow could be seen winging a solitary cawing flight out over a Canadian cornfield on the other side of the river.

Do you know that we have two crows? There is the garden variety, *Corvus brachyrhynchos,* and then there is *Corvus ossifragus,* the fish crow. This fellow is a denizen of the foreshore, the waterfront, and the salt-water marsh. A smaller job he is, best recognized by his more nasal *car* with a flat *a* in contrast with the *caw* with a broad *a* of his more familiar cornfed cousin.

At night I do not bother to set any alarm. For in the morning at getting up time, the crows will be in caucus, and I prefer to be awakened in that manner.

Summer

This summer afternoon is hot and the air is humid as I cross the Canal and roll down the causeway that traverses Thousand Acre Marsh. A diversity of greens lies on each side of the road, the deep lush green of thick growing millet on the one hand, and the yellow-green of waving feather grass on the other. As always the marsh is alive with birds—dipping swallows kissing dimples in the water, blackbirds that zoom toward me with their scarlet shoulders ablaze, a parcel of small ducks that I take to be blue-winged teal, paddling and feeding in a cove and long-legged blue heron standing at regular intervals like solemn sentinels. At the clap of my hands—a gesture I can never resist when I see a crane—the nearest one launches itself into ungainly flight dragging its long legs behind. Then as the next pond opens up amid the marsh grass, I ease to the side of the road and come to a stop.

On the far shore a tumultuous riot of pink and white hibiscus—marsh mallows as they are called by many—is intermingled with patches of the deep purple of loosestrife. This galaxy of wild pink and purple is the backdrop and the pool in front is the stage. There, tall, slender, and nervously alert upon long stiltlike legs, stands a snow-white egret.

The water in the pool is placid, so calm that I can see the green millet and the blossoms on the far shore standing in a reverse reflection. There are, as it were, two marshes, one above and the other below the surface. And when the egret, launching into easy flight, flaps its great white wings, they seem to touch at the surface the great white wings of its mirrored reflection.

These birds startle the eye as here and there in a sweeping glance over the marsh I glimpse their graceful snow-white shapes against the green. In one sector I count nine of them, and beyond at the edge of the marsh on the bare branches of a dead tree sit three more. Through the glasses I watch them as they wade on their long black legs, and one meticulously clutched step after another carries the long outstretched neck and yellow bill forward toward the prey until at the end of a swift thrust a hapless frog disappears. In high flight the falling sun bathes their white bodies with a warm light.

Now I watch two settling into a far cove. So low do they fly that I see only the tips of their long wings above and in the openings of the tall grass. Now and again through the still air of early twilight there comes the low hoarse croak that is their cry.

All the while I am here there is one standing on a log in the near foreground, hunched over and curiously still. Perhaps it is asleep. Around the log are duck, feeding, quacking, swimming, and preening, and the old white one has a distinctly magisterial air as he presides over them.

On this summer day at sunset the egrets have taken over Thousand Acre Marsh.

With the sinking of the sun on another July day, across the sky about halfway to the zenith, there stretches from northeast to southwest a long bank of white cloud. It hangs there undisturbed by any wind, its uppermost edge tinged with golden yellow. This is the afterglow. But the more remarkable thing is the quality of the light all about me on the ground, and it is obvious that this great cloud bank is serving as a gigantic reflector.

On taking a turn in this transplanted light I notice first how the butt ends of the red oak logs in the woodpile are almost golden. At the edge of the woods stands an old stump. The dry rot in its side glows with a deep reddish brown. The trunks of the Lombardy poplars, nondescript in the daytime, are of a deep gray showing every fissure of the bark in clear-cut outline. A red tin roof gives off a tinge of deep vermilion that contrasts sharply with the liquid blue-green—the color of a breaking wave after a storm—that shines from the clapboards of the water tower rising above the roof. Hard by a stone wall reveals unsuspected colors in the facing of the stones. The green of the trees—maple, oak, poplar, beech, dogwood and the evergreens—each now has its own tone and a shade peculiar to it alone.

Aloft where the sky is marked off by the golden edge of the cloud it is of a clear sapphire blue. And below a three-quarters moon shines palely through the transparent, faint olive-green veil of the cloud. So it is for the short space of a quarter hour before this transplanted light wanes and dies in this small segment of the globe.

But the event of this country evening comes later when the breathless quiet of the hot July night lies brooding over the earth. Suddenly the silence is shattered. Sharp, shrill, and somewhere between a sneeze and a snort, it brings me to my feet in a quick search for the flashlight.

Outside the moon is down under and the night impenetrably dark. The darkness over the meadow is here and there spotted by the sudden sparks of the fireflies. Then comes that snort again and the flashlight snaps on. Just above the level of the growing corn a pair of molten eyes is caught in the white beam. This is the doe, and once again comes the shrill snort. And then the sight of sights as two glowing coals rise and fall in sudden arcs tracing out in the darkness the unseen path of the bounding buck.

At midnight all sound is from afar. The sudden call of some hidden night bird arises in the depth of the woods. The faint barking of a distant dog comes borne from an unseen barnyard. A harsh shriek of locked brakes comes from a faraway highway. High and muted the piping signal of some unseen ship out on the river is echoed seconds later by the whistle of that other ship that passes in the night and speaks the first in passing.

This night is rich in odors. In the calm cool air at midnight I walk from one perfumed zone into another as the pungent smell of fresh-mown hay is succeeded by the faint fragrance of blooming honeysuckle, to be in turn eclipsed by the mingled odors of the rose garden.

At midnight all that is familiar has a shadowed reality. The skyline of the towering trees shoulders high into the sky and patches of light gleam amid the leaves reflecting the glow of distant street lights on the horizon. The black bulk of the water tower above the stable is darkly ominous. Here and there the silent sparks that are the fireflies come on to gleam and then to die away above the invisible meadow. And over all is the deep dark firmament studded with the stabs of light that are the stars.

The clamor of one day has dissipated, that of the next is yet to arise. A walk at midnight on such a night is an experience in living. It may be had by the mere effort, by oneself and alone.

For those whose rest is fitful on these breathlessly quiet summer nights, there comes with the approach of dawn a restful prelude to the day's stint in a work-a-day world. After I have lain hot, tossing, and restless through the still night, then it is that the birds herald the growth of light in a darkened world. Beyond the windows in the woods, in the shrubbery, and in the fields there are birds—birds galore. With the first paling of the eastern sky there arise their faint chirpings and callings, scattered and sporadic at first, but gradually increasing in volume until soon they are giving forth a chorus. Then the prima donnas give voice.

There is that lusty lunged warbler whose vibrant cry of *teacher, teacher*—and then in increasing intensity—TEACHER, TEACHER—has earned him the soubriquet of the teacher bird. Often I hear but rarely see this bird whose proper name, the ovenbird, derives from its nest on the ground that is arched over like a Dutch oven. In the pause for breath that follows this song, there peals from afar within the depths of the woods the deep, liquid, flutelike notes of the wood thrush— *ee-o—lay*. Next comes the clear whistling note that in a descending scale gives its name to the veery. As the growing light of the false dawn dissipates the shades of departing night, these three, a warbler and two thrushes, sing over and over, and again and again, their vibrant roles against the chorus of the lesser songbirds. Then with the rise of the sun their singing almost suddenly ceases. The chorus diminishes and soon I hear only the sporadic note of some solitary bird.

Deep within the dark green of the rhododendrons a triple-pronged yoke supports a hidden robin's nest. A sturdy affair, stoutly contrived of dried coarse grass, it survives the seasons and when relined in the spring of the year, furnishes a niche for the new fledglings. So handy to the house is it that I had a

ringside seat for this early summer tragedy. More than that—
by chance I became a participant.

The first thing I noticed, while seated at the desk in du-
bious contemplation of the month's bills, was a curious
irregular tapping like the clatter of a distant typewriter. The
source of the sound remains inexplicable. Perhaps it had no
connection with what was coming. But at any rate it so held
my attention that I was instantly drawn from my chair by the
sudden anguished outcries of the birds. Outside the door the
air over the rhododendrons was alive with fluttering robins
who flashed into and out of the leaves filling the air with
their cries. There must have been a half dozen of them dart-
ing in and out of the bushes. I stepped to the corner of the
house where a view within the rhododendrons was possible.
Then I saw.

In a horrible festooning there looped down from branch to
branch the slithering body of a blacksnake. Within its jaws
there struggled a fledgling robin. There hurtled at the snake
through the branches a robin, wings beating, beak agape.
Then came another and another, as in a slow uncoiling the
snake slid slowly toward the earth.

What to do? The gun was on the rack. The shells were
stowed. I made a dash, retrieved the gun, ran to where a box
of shells was cached, fumbling found a number five, and
emerged again still on the run out the back door and around
the house toward the other side of the rhododendrons, for I
figured that the snake would make toward the woods. The
robins were still circling the nest in a flurry of alarm. Then
almost underfoot in the narrow path through the honeysuckle, an untoward motion caught my eye.

There it was turning this way and that, lazily, in the warm
sun. About a quarter of the way down there was an unpleas-

ant bulge. The gun did the rest and there was naught of it left alive save the quivering tail that does not die, some say, until sundown. The report fetched the setter on the run and he took a great interest in the twitching tail, as also did a couple of neighbors who came from a nearby field to talk over the event and pass their comment.

Soon all was quiet. The robins scattered. Later I slipped out into the depths of the rhododendrons. There on the nest sat the female robin. And seeing me she nervously took flight.

Often am I put in mind of the summer shower I once beat to shelter on a clear July day. As a phenomenon of nature a shower cannot be appreciated where you wear rubbers, carry an umbrella, and insist on a mackintosh. For then you are city-bound, hemmed about by the strictures of civilized living. A fellow gets just as wet from the rain bouncing back from the pavements as he does when it first falls out of the sky. And generally there is no place to watch it or listen to it. It just drives down, splashes back and gets you all wet twice.

We were lazying, my companion and I, on the pine-clad bank of a pond after a cooling swim and a box lunch. It was clear, the sun shone, and a steady breeze was soughing through the needles over our heads and lapping little waves against the stones. Now a clustered cumulus that a short time before had been just another cloud drifting before the southwest breeze began to loom large in the west, to darken at its base, and to take on an ominous aspect. We took to the canoe, paddled quickly to the head of the pond, and got on the carry. For in the next pond of the chain there was a camp and for this we headed on the run.

There the wind had risen and it came in puffs. At first it was hard going upwind but with a turn of the shore line, it came on the quarter and we drove along before it, quartering the waves and easing the canoe into their troughs. By now the sky was darkening rapidly and the tops of the trees on the ridges were thrashing and lying over with the wind. We paddled hard to win this race with the wind and rain. On high ground rising from a ledge stood the shelter, and with the canoe quickly overturned we made it on the run just as the first drops stung our bare backs. The cabin was sheathed but breast high so we could look out all around.

With the coming of the rain the wind dropped and the surface of the pond was dotted with widening dimples that grew closer and closer together. A steady pattering rose and rose until it became a roar, and then the surface became a vast collection of tiny cups of water thrown up from the pond by the driving rain. There burst a sudden single clap of thunder. Overhead on the roof was a roaring tattoo. Outside the spruces and the balsams were dripping ceaselessly. I held my dipper out into the rain and quickly caught enough for a drink. The far shore grew obscure and dim. And so it was for a spell—a straight downpouring of endlessly falling rain.

Then imperceptibly it slackened. The roaring lessened. The little cups on the surface subsided. Of a sudden the shower was gone. We could hear it drumming in the leaves on the next ridge and we saw it in slow motion—a wall of rain retreating slowly into the next valley. The sun came out. The whitethroats reappeared and recommenced their singing to one another. And we went swimming again just to celebrate the occasion.

It was on a midsummer day that a sudden commotion in the growth by the roadside brought me up with a round turn. Then I saw her. Half hidden in the greenery of the asparagus patch from whence came a frenzy of startled clucking was the brown mottled body of a hen pheasant. I took a step toward her. Immediately the honeysuckle into which I had stepped came alive with little round feathered bodies, the size of baby chicks, that scuttered here and scattered there. Ten of the tiny creatures there were—a nye of pheasants.

One little creature was almost underfoot. Leaning over I cupped my hands in front of him and in alarm he leaped into the trap. For a split second I felt him, soft and crouching, his black eyes blinking, a little feathered parcel of perfected camouflage with a slight yellow bar on his wings. Then with a sudden spurt he slipped through my fingers and scrambled off into the depth of the honeysuckle. That young one, I figured, would live to grow up.

Standing still I watched. The parting and swaying of the tops of the tall weeds betrayed the path of the hen as she slipped through them, emitting a steady stream of alarmed clucking. Now and again a sharp wiry squeaking bespoke the response of one of her brood. Occasionally I glimpsed her walking very like a long-tailed hen with a chick or two in the van. The nye was being rounded up. As I stood there in flew a goldfinch to alight on the swinging top of a tall stalk of wild lettuce. A spangle of golden yellow and black, he swayed back and forth unconcernedly pecking at the lettuce seeds, oblivious to the domestic turbulence that went on deep in the weeds beneath him.

A month later to a day, a familiar low clucking called me out into the corn patch. There they were again—no mistake about it. Directly the rustle of the leaves betrayed my creeping passage, and the old hen began her familiar decoying tactics. Keeping close by in the row in front of me, she endeavored to entice me by short spurts away from her hidden brood. But it did not work too well. For the young setter had come along for the ride and his wet nose led him off to the other side of the patch. Then of a sudden they began to explode—the first one almost underfoot, then another in the far corner, next two at once, and then three. The air was alive with pheasant scaling out and over the top of the corn and on in short flight into the woods at the edge of the patch. This was a moment of sheer sport.

It was their size that struck me, by now that of plump spring chickens. My count revealed the whole ten of them, and by now they were of a size to keep clear of the foxes. Come the opening day of the season this nye would be scattered all over Brandywine Hundred but this hardly deterred me from getting down the old gun for a good going over with oil and rag.

Once a hurricane has blown itself out there is ushered in an aftermath of power and beauty. At the shore there is the surf ceaselessly assaulting the beach in great rolling combers, the crests of which are torn by the offshore wind into streamers of spray flying back like the manes of wild sea horses. Up ashore there are the streams and rivers which, filled by the torrential rain of hour after hour, pour and plunge headlong through their appointed courses. So it was along the Brandywine.

By midafternoon the river was really rolling—and still rising. There was that peculiar dank smell in the air that always rises out of a stream when a freshet is running. Due to the tide which, hidden beneath the swift moving head of water, was making, the surface roared by in regular swells with the surges below breaking upstream into spuming white water. "When them sheep start jumping upstream," says the experienced canoeman, "it's time to go ashore and lug."

I watched the butt of a log, two feet at least in diameter, toss by like a tumbling cork. Then there were three black-birds riding a log downstream like sombre river drivers. When it fetched up with a bump in a mass of flotsam, caught and held fast by a tree, they left it in startled flight. And as the overflowing river flowed out a colony of red ants, some of them climbed up my trouser legs. For a few moments the remainder clustered in a crawling multitude at the top of some long grass until the rising river swept them away to unseen destruction.

Out where the Twelve Mile Circle crosses the Brandywine the road parallels it and here the rise had flowed out the meadows. Instead of a placid riband of water winding quietly between tree-lined banks, there was a great long lake with an island in the middle of it where a knoll supported a clump of trees. At the edges masses of black-eyed Susans presented an unaccustomed aspect of small water lilies. The entrance to a country estate looked like a Japanese garden with the water up over the road and close to the top of the stone wall, sur-rounding the entrance posts and stretching out across the pasture toward the farm buildings.

At a later stage this great head of water would produce dramatic effects downstream. And so, come midnight when the freshet was at its height, I took my stand in the dark valley at the foot of Breck's Lane. Here, with the narrow tor-rent roaring through the spillway on the near side and sweep-ing on the far side of the mill in a vast descending surge over the dam, there was presented a scene of unbelievable power and beauty. A smooth path of dark power, bending in beau-tiful contour, suddenly erupted into a surging, tossing, whirl-ing spume of white water. Each watery convolution held my gaze spellbound in a fascination of contemplation.

This freshet was the answer to the eternal prayer of the

canoeman—for plenty of water, water so swift and so strong that his canoe will stand no more. Then he may speed swiftly downstream choosing his course with the sure instinct that is born of experience, setting it by deft twists and sudden strong strokes of the paddle through the swiftest rips, while the shores on either hand, in ever variant contour and from an angle unknown to those who plod them afoot or by automobile, present a shifting kaleidoscope of natural beauty.

On the second day of this freshet my companion and I put in at Lenape. Three hours later we hauled out at Rockland. In between was an unforgettable experience.

We enjoyed again the strange fascination of sliding down an inclined plane that is the treasured experience of all canoemen. As the stream stretched away from bend to bend, it appeared to the approaching eye to incline sharply, and down this in our slight craft we slid swiftly. The shores lined with overhanging willows and noble sycamores and supporting stands of oak, beech, and maple that here and there rose on the ridges; how different they were from the pine, balsam and hackmatack of a northern stream. In one place we followed the river in its course through a grove of such trees.

At another juncture we heard first the roar of white water and then, around the next bend, we saw those "white sheep" trying to leap upstream over an old mill dam. This would be too much for our little fifteen-footer so we passed to one side through the ancient millrace to shoot with sheer excitement the white waters of the rip made by the remains of the smaller lower dam. This was it—what we had come for.

The birds of the Brandywine are a rich experience. Upstream in the meadows it is a blackbirds' stream. At each bend, seemingly, a blue heron would sweep on before us on undulating wing and I once saw three in the air at once.

There were bitterns galore. Duck—black, mallard, and the summer duck—rose before us to turn and swing back high above the trees. And once in a flash of scarlet flame a tanager flew swiftly out of and back into an overhanging oak. Or could it have been the rare vermilion flycatcher, for in midair it snapped up a fly.

Then toward the end as we drifted slowly in the deadwater formed by the dam at Rockland, we came upon a colony of egrets—five of them and obviously a family, for three were quite small. In the still wet meadow they stalked on their long black legs until, alarmed by our stealthy approach behind a clump of willows, they launched aloft into slow flight that carried their white-pinioned bodies, gliding without other visible motion against the green hillside, to an abrupt alighting at a safer distance.

The sky is overcast and showers threaten as I approach my first port of call, the town of New Castle. With a lift of the spirit I note that it is girt upon three sides with hibiscus-haunted marshes where those great pink and white flowers, wide open on this overcast day, spot the expanses of green. Here I pause to procure the loan of a knife, having been thus reminded that I should not return empty-handed from my excursion. Out in front of the town the surface of the river is gray—an undercast to the overcast sky.

The rolling river country that slopes gently down to merge with the Delaware River at its western shore is traversed by a narrow winding road long known as the River Road. I lazy along it, traveling in a lane bordered by the light blue blossoms of wild chicory—on past Red Lion Creek where on the bridge the ubiquitous fisherman wets his line with patient certainty and the carp leap aloft in arcs of shining silver.

Here white lily pads lie upon the surface of calm dark pools. Now and again a vista—in the olden books a visto—opens up to the distant river where a freighter is revealed creeping seaward. The clarion call of a hidden bobwhite rings in my ears, and hard by in a low field a red-wing blackbird shutters his red-gold epaulettes in a fluttering alighting on a swaying reed. In the golden stubble of fresh-cut wheat myriads of blackbirds flash their black bodies like living coals and rising in a revolving constellation descend to alight in a neighboring cornfield. Then for a time the tossing of tasseled corn is on either hand. And this is succeeded by hedges that are alive with the flame of trumpet flowers. At length the rain commences—a drizzle drozzle that soon becomes a steady slanting sprinkle.

Next the Canal is crossed and I roll out onto the causeway that traverses Thousand Acre Marsh. In the first expanse that opens up there is a border of deep purple, a profusion of loosestrife. Beyond lies acre after acre of marsh spotted with the great white and pink blossoms of hibiscus, and then again a distant border of deep purple. In the far distance lie the green of the millet, the open water, and the misty skyline. Rolling to a stop alongside this great flower garden of Nature, I listen to the sweet strain of a song sparrow, repeated again and again as if in endless celebration of this expanse of beauty. A breeze brings the fresh moist scent-laden air of the marsh.

Then on down the causeway as a kingfisher flashes past, a minnow in its beak. In a pool I count the fat bodies of twenty-one black duck standing all hunched up in the rain. White egrets stand like white sentinels against the deep green of the millet. A small shore bird—a lesser yellowleg perhaps—displays a flashing whiteness of rump as it hovers a foot or so above the mud and then settles to stalk about and feed.

On the far side of the causeway in a clump of small trees is the event of the forenoon. The leaves are alive with fluttering, twittering birds. I note that the branches are laden with ripe chokecherries of a deep black purple. The leaves are all aflutter in the breeze and the air is all aflutter with the birds. After I take my stand with my field glasses, they show no fear, soaring, skimming, diving, and then hovering in a frenzy of fluttering amid the leaves to alight and rest. They are a countless horde. Scarce a dozen feet away the backs of the males show a deep burnished blue, a black cap, and undersides of the purest white. Tree swallows they are—a myriad of them.

At length I put about, not failing to fill the back of the car with great folds of the purple loosestrife and the pink and the white hibiscus that I may reward my neighbor of the knife and myself enjoy the opening and the shutting of these remarkable blossoms each day for a week.

On the devilishly hot nights that curse this country in midsummer a man needs to do more than merely get cool. What he really needs is to find some sea room and give his spirit a few moments ease. It is the only way that he can wash the sweat out of his soul. Time was when I could do this on the upper deck of the New Castle Ferry ploughing across the Delaware River and making her own night breeze. But all that is gone now. Nonetheless I can still get the solace that I need.

A shore line is always a boundary between two worlds. On the Battery down in New Castle I can put the town and its lights and its people, together with my office and the day's work, in back of me and look down and out over the broad reaches of the Delaware River. Here on the stillest and the hottest of nights, the air out on the river and the air ashore are in the slightest conflict, and I can count on this evanescent pulse and repulse of motion to cool me off.

As my eyes accustom to the darkness the distant shores of Jersey and lower Delaware emerge on either hand in shadowed form. Then there are lights—red lights that warn the airman of the height of the St. Georges span and the invisible towers of the bridge over the Canal below Delaware City. Fixed and flashing white lights both beckon and warn the seafarer on his passage upstream into the interior and again downstream to the ocean and the outer world. Now a winking alternation of red and white lights sweeping in a high passage eastward betrays the path of flight. And of a sudden in the western sky a flood of brilliant white light bespeaks the approach to a landing at the airport.

A low muttering roar sounds behind and I turn. In slow motion a truck is crawling across the park emitting a vast cloud of white vapor, thereby assuring to the inhabitants of New Castle a night free of mosquitoes. By now the little town is hidden and from behind the white curtain there comes its distant sounds—a dog barking, the banging of a door, the low murmur of traffic.

To the river again. A cluster of bright lights is moving steadily downstream. The slight breeze brings the noises of the ship—the distant churning of machinery, the clang of iron upon iron as an unsecured door slats and slats again against a bulkhead, the splash and splatter of the bilges being pumped overside. The light of the moon filters through the overcast. The stack and cranes of the freighter are dimly to be seen. Soon there comes close at hand the rasp on the sand that is the wash of her wake. Her lights dim in the distance as she furrows her way to the sea. Perhaps her first port of call will be in Iceland. The thought gives me a pleasant shiver.

Here on the Battery between two worlds—that of the Delaware country and that of the other outer world—a man may seek his ease on a hot summer night.

The State of Maine

To span within the compass of a day the distance between the middle Atlantic state that is Delaware, and the state farthest down east that is the State of Maine is an experience that to me always savors of a miracle. The reason lies in the contrast between this day with its five-hundred-mile journey so swiftly traversed, and the day of those summer vacations of long years ago when it took all day in a horse-drawn carriage, moving at a snail's pace in the ruts of a sandy road, to arrive at the shore in the late afternoon with a distance run of a scant twenty miles.

Why—I am often asked—is it always the State of Maine, and why do you go down east? The answers are easy and traditional. In the early days you went by sea from Boston, when traveling to Maine. And you set your course due east. Then with the prevailing winds you sailed downwind, and hence you went down east. As for the State of Maine, the phrase is in line of direct descent from the District of Maine of revolutionary times and the Province of Maine of colonial times, the name Maine deriving from the early seventeenth century use of the word "main" to connote the mainland. This usage still exists alongshore as when island folk are heard to speak of going over to the main.

From west to east the coast of the State of Maine is traversed by a series of rugged promontories. They lie between river and river and they stretch far down into the sea. These and the islands beyond them in ranges that are roughly parallel mark the courses of the glaciers of the ice age that once ploughed deep channels far out on the continental shelf.

One of these fir-crowned promontories lies between the New Meadows River and Casco Bay on the west and the Kennebec on the east. At its terminus there are all the riches the Maine coast has to offer—marshes that stretch their widening vistas between fir-lined ridges and through which little salt rivers wander in tortuous curves on their way to the sea, a granite pine-clad mountain, deep coves at every turn of the road, fresh-water ponds hidden deep within the woods yet hard by the sea, a headland that is thick with hardwood and evergreen growth ending abruptly in sheer cliff, a ledge-lined point jutting far out into the Atlantic, a great broad long flat beach and in the distance the dome of an island broken by its lighthouse.

In the early evening of my arrival I sit out on the veranda. These verandas always have the same kind of chairs. The seats are of rush and they cock up against the wall of the cottage as a chair should, comfortable and easylike. This veranda looks out from a small bluff, and it gives upon a variant scene. In the foreground a little salt river sweeps seaward now pouring the dregs of the tide out of a marsh. Across this little stream the beach extends, curving eastward in a slow and steady sweep to clasp within its thus rounded bight a crescent of the sea. Here there rise out of the depths of the brown sand the ancient and blackened timbers of a coastwise schooner once cast up on this lee shore. Beyond there are the lines of white that are the breaking waves, forming and re-forming in tune with the muted and distant sound of the sea. Alongshore there are the dunes, low and rounding, and beyond them, across the flat level of the marsh that they enclose, there rise in the distance the darkening sides of the distant ridges topped with jagged skylines of pointed firs.

Up over this scene of shore and sea there float on still

wings the gulls. They scale out of the sky in back of the house, appearing suddenly in the air by the edge of the veranda roof to soar on set wings silently out over the beach. The sun is down. The light of the afterglow is dying in the pools of water left on the beach by the receding tide. Around the horizon lights are beginning to wink—beacons that mark some unseen ledge, winking on, winking off. Then there is the light that studs the darkening summit of the island of Seguin like a great yellow jewel.

This first evening I sit out on the veranda cocked up in my comfortable chair, and I watch while the shadows lengthen and the light fades and at length fails and darkness comes on. The air grows chill and the sound of the distant surf whispers softly from far across the wet sand. For a long time I sit thus, for it is a pleasant and restful thing just to sit, cocked up in a chair on a veranda, within sight and earshot of the sea, and let the daylight fade and darkness come on. It is always this way —this first evening at the shore.

Time was, and it was not so long ago, when mankind marked well both sunrise and sunset. This was when a man's work was from sunup to sundown. Even today in certain exigencies, haying for example, the day's work will cover an even greater compass. In my time I have seen men and their teams start in slow motion across the fields long before light and have listened to the whirr and the clatter of their mowing machine coming from the dim end of the same fields long after dark.

In our state of habitual indifference to this great mystery of nature, the scattered occasions when we have been up with the sun are vivid tablets in the storehouse of the memory. And just as the greater beauty of a sunset is revealed in the glory of the afterglow, so in reverse the mysterious promise of the light that is to come, that some falsely call the false dawn, is the greater beauty of the sunrise. Then as the earth rolls eastward on its axis, the horizon where sky meets sea is edged with light that grows, broadens, deepens, and extends upward with the watching.

Suddenly this thus enlightened canopy is filled with color. The fillets of the mackerel sky are tinged with shades of pink that glow and fade and then glow again. Below, the familiar contours of marsh, beach, rocks, sea, and island have emerged. Then for a matter of long and memorable moments, colors pass and repass as if reflected from some great hidden kaleidoscope. On the beach one shade of brown succeeds another. The rocks are now dun, now gray, and now black. The sea is a vast panoply whereon a spectrum of shifting colors forms and re-forms—slate blue, dark green, and rich purple, each merging with the other. Now the horizon glows with gold. The moment is at hand. A slice of yellow light emerges out of the sea. The sun is up.

This miracle transpires in a deep and unbroken silence. Even the sea seems stilled for this moment of the dawn. Only there are murmurs in the air of the ancient phrases of the classics—of the rosy-fingered dawn and a wine-colored sea.

I commence my walk on the beach eastward toward the ascending sun. A chill west wind assaults my back as I wade through the ice-cold water of the small salt river. Directly ahead and marked and earmarked at a tremendous distance by the uniform color and flat expanse of the sand, there rise up the black ribs and worn stem of the wreck. For a generation now the bare bones of this skeleton have stuck up out of the sand to be submerged by each day's tides. In sharp contrast to this sepulcher there is parked above the tide line in the shelter of a dune a graceful monoplane standing lightly on the sand like a great dragonfly.

The beach stretches ahead in endless expanse as I traverse the damp foreshore where the sweeping waves are wafting up tiny ridges of white foam. The myriad bubbles of this foam sparkle with iridescence. The birds are in abundance—shore birds that rise as I approach, sweep out over the whitening surf in a living constellation, wheel against the volute of a wave, and then sweep in to settle on the shore again, where they first pursue a receding sea and then run away from its oncoming successor, feeding always on the run. Gulls too, a myriad of them, fleck the brown sand with their gray and white forms. I clap my hands and then the beach is bare as, flapping, they fill the air with their ponderous bodies and screaming outcries.

Two miles of this and I plunge naked into the depths of the next little salt river. Then the return, this time with the sun warming my back, and with what an appetite for the steaming bowl of fish chowder that awaits me.

At night I stand again upon the wooded headland looking eastward at the sea. This headland is unusual, even unique. It rises sheer to a considerable height and to its rocky base there makes up the great flat wide beach. Where I stand a single small oak marks the center of a visto that has been cut to lead the eye out to sea.

Below, the broad expanse of sand lies bare and dark, yet I can see outlined in shadow there—the tide being at the ebb —the now uncovered mouth of the little river coursing in its long slow curve out into the sea. The flatness of the beach and the emergence of the stream cause the waves to multiply their tumbling, and in consequence the sound of the sea comes in a distant monotonous roar that is louder than ordinarily. Beyond, a mile and more distant across the dark sea, there looms in shrouded contour the great mound of the island. Here, exactly amidships, as it were, a large white light stands at the skyline. This is the fixed white light on Seguin, and on the foreshore in the wash left by the endlessly receding seas I see it in image, palely reflected.

Up above this panorama of beach and sea and island across a sky that is mottled with dark clouds, there sails on its endless course the great white full moon. At the moment of my watching it gleams opaque through the thin rim of a cloud and, as always, it is the cloud that seems to be motionless and the moon to sail like some ship of the air. Below in the foreground on the surface of the sea lies the shadow of this cloud, and here the sea is dark and almost unseen, but beyond in the open water past Seguin and the three blunt ledges that flank it inshore—the Herons—the moonlight dances in brilliance on the waters. There is the reflected path of the sailing moon.

This moonlit patch of the sea is historic. Here between the mouth of the Kennebec and the island of Seguin with Monhegan in the far background, near a century and a half ago on the brilliantly sunlit day of September 5, 1813, there were to be seen shortly after noon two brigs, each maneuvering to gain the weather gauge of the other in the smart westerly breeze that would freshen in the early afternoon. This was the opening of the celebrated sea fight between the *Enterprise* and the *Boxer* in the course of which their youthful captains—Burrows and Blyth, each in his early twenties— would fall on their own quarterdecks. Today they lie in adjoining graves in the old Eastern Cemetery in Portland, as will be well remembered by those who recall Longfellow's "My Lost Youth."

This night too is clear. Afar down east at the regular inter-vals of a minute, there can be seen at first a pale gleam, the mere promise of a light, and then for a few seconds' duration the white light of the occulting beam of the lighthouse on Monhegan.

"When 'tis clear like this," says one, "and you can see these lights, it's a weather breeder."

And so, as the old logs were wont to put it, the next day starts with fog and a light rain. Brought in by a southerly and this is to be a gray day. It is a day of quiet and repose when small sounds are more than ordinarily noticeable as I sit alone in the spacious living room that looks out over and down upon the sea. There is the even *tick-tock, tick-tock* of the old clock on the mantel, the soft snap of a small fire, the hushed rushing of the breeze through the leaves of the scrub oaks, and the murmuring sound of the distant sea. All hori-zons are now lost and the edges of familiar things are in-distinct.

I am awakened before dawn the next day by a great con-course of gulls. They raise an extraordinary clamor. It is in-cessant and the mixture of their raucous callings is so blended as to form a cacophonous chorus. Nonetheless against this there now and again rises a single voice that is unmistakable —the shrieking of an individual gull. This fellow makes his own music and steps to his own tune.

In the dim light before dawn they have foregathered where the river winds between the sand flats in its last turn before it courses over the beach into the sea. The water is dotted black with their great forms. The banks are lined with them, squatting, waddling, and forever screaming. The cacophony is the hailing cry for others who heed the com-munal cries. I watch them fly in, ponderously winging over the surface of the river coming in from the sea. Above and from in back of the cottage on the bluff they scale into sight above the trees, set their wings, and drop down out of the sky to drop their feet on the sand and join this caravanserai. From far up the beach they wing and out of the dusky distance where the marsh lies they come in droves.

The uproar is ceaseless. Single gulls will run the four steps, rise, and then drop again. Others unfold their broad wings, stretch them and then as if upon second thought, fold them again carefully on their rumps. Now and again two of them will go to fighting. A favorite gambit is to rush, wings spread wide, neck outstretched and beak agape, plucking at the tail of some luckless opponent, who flees screaming on the run. Above in the river I see outlined against the water the tall form of a blue heron. In his hunt for the sand eels he stalks about, unconcerned with the medley.

Beyond the caucus of the gulls the eastern horizon lightens. At first the jagged tips of the firs are outlined in pink. Above is the deep blue of the paling night. In a few moments the growing light reveals over the marsh a low blanket of white mist. And then there is a remarkable and, for those few fleeting moments, a memorable sight. Through and above this white mist there rise the tops of the dunes and the gnarled limbs of the scrub pines that have grown and died there—a disembodied scene that seems to float in the air.

Of a sudden a glint of gold is above the skyline. Then as if by a common accord the raucous outcries of the assembled gulls cease abruptly. And now they are all in flight, winging in different directions. The day is on.

In the line of a gull's flight just to the south of west and twenty odd miles distant from this Small Point Beach, on the western coast of Maine there is a great bay enclasped by the outstretched arms of Cape Elizabeth and Prouts Neck. Here there fronts the sea a coast line in varied aspect of ledge and rock piled before high points, of salt river and marsh, and beaches in sweeping arcs of white sand. To the eastward there rises the low dome of Richmond's Island, an ancient landfall and fishing station, visited by Champlain and named the Isle de Bacchus nearly two decades before Plymouth. Broad off in front lies a ledge to which early charts long ago gave the magnificent name of The Old Proprietor. To the westward there juts the rock-lined promontory that is Prouts Neck.

Within the bight of the curving strand of sand that has long been known as Scarborough Beach, and rising from the edge of the sea beyond the grass-covered dunes, there is a slight height of land. Here at the edge of a grove of white pine a long rambling structure has faced the Gulf of Maine for upwards of a century. This is the Atlantic House.

Before breakfast at a summer hotel the world is one's oyster. No one else is astir save the night watchman, who wishes he were not, and the kitchen people, who are busy with their tasks. I walk blinking into the strong light of an early summer sun to find the dew sparkling on webs of gossamer. Down through the quiet dunes and the rustling beach grass I go until there stretches forth before me a broad expanse of hard-packed sand that, at the end of the foreshore, merges with the sparkling blue sea, and then my eyes sweep on until they meet the taut line of the horizon.

The encircling arms of the two rock-bound points enclose in a cove a long slow curve of yellow sand. I face to the westward and I walk. Underfoot the sand is firm, cool, and still damp from the ebb of the tide. Just beyond the line of the small surf a black head rises slowly and a pair of eyes, dripping, eye me with complete unconcern. Then into the crest of the next wave, a seal withdraws. A crow wings, calling harshly, in over the dunes. A gull wings silently overhead. As I traverse the foreshore the shore birds precede me in little arcs of flight out over the flowing tide. And then before I know it, I have done my mile. This now is the moment. This is it.

The first step into that blue, blue sea is cold—cold. At ebb tide and in the early morning, it must be in the upper fifties. I plunge on in, the worst of it coming when the water hits me amidships. In that instant I cleave the curve of a wave to emerge with a rush on the other side. Instantly a swift glow of well-being surges through my every part. I start for the shore on the run, and as always when I was a small boy, I make it a race with the wave that rushes shoreward behind me in swift pursuit. And just as then, sometimes I win, and sometimes I lose.

I have stood at the water's edge on this same beach on a sultry day in August. I could not stand up ashore where the hot sand burned my feet. Nor was it any use to bathe. The water was lukewarm and after a plunge the rays of the sun filtering through those thick layers of haze burned my wet flesh cruelly—even dangerously. The air by the sea was just as hot and just as oppressive as it was up ashore.

Then all of a sudden it happened. A blast of chilled fresh air struck my bare chest—a Labradorean breeze that had coasted far over the cool Atlantic on past Newfoundland and Nova Scotia across the Gulf of Maine on its way to this foreshore. For a delicious instant I lived in a split world. My chest was chilled while my back was still aflame with the heat. Then it enveloped me and passed on up ashore. Now

I lived again and leaped alive in the cool bracing sea air.

A sea turn is what they call this, and upon occasion I have even seen one come ashore.

That morning the early light had been of a pale yellow. This was due to the angling effect of the sun's rays shining through the heavy haze that hung everywhere. It betokened another day of heat, of lifeless air, of high humidity—known in these parts in the early days of August as another dog day. As I drove upcountry across the sand plains of the valley of the Saco, the gravelly and sandy surface of the sphere tossed back its burning heat into my face. In any one of the many valleys of the rivers that course out of the height of land in the northern part of Maine down into the sea, a dog day in early August is a searing experience.

I was on my way back in the late afternoon when I saw that cold front coming ashore about ten miles from the coast. From the horizon where the hidden ocean lay, the sky stretched upward like a great gray pall. Suddenly there came into the air a freshness, a coolness, and a new vitality, and in that instant in the distance on either hand there were to be seen pale gray ghosts drifting slowly in over the land, obscuring the ridges and wooded hillsides. Later, when the sea came in view, there lay along the horizon like a vast billow of curled cotton, a fog bank. Then looking back I could see its advance guards marching up into that baked and parched area known as upcountry. I had been witness to a sea turn.

Scarborough Bar is handy on the one hand to the sea and on the other to a great salt marsh. It is the fortunate effluvium of five small salt rivers that with each tide fill and then drain the Scarborough Marshes. At the mouth of these converging streams, as the tide ebbs, there is slowly laid bare a vast stretch of white sand—a place for memorable walking.

To come upon it I first pass through a stretch of low dune thick with long-leaved marsh grass in which clumps of dusty miller give off their pearl-gray sheen. Here the red, white, and blue, and purple blossoms of the beach pea still spot the grass. Also I pass a clump of beach plum, its branches loaded thick with round green promises of red and purple fruit.

There is a pause in the soft sand to kick off my sneakers, for barefoot is the only way to traverse a bar. Then the sand is cool and firm to the foot. Out beyond the bar the can and nun buoys marking the mouth of the river strain seaward at a steep angle in the swift ebb, and toward one of these a fleet of sloops is bearing down with spinnakers blossoming out into small clouds of white canvas.

On this Scarborough Bar there are birds galore—flying, walking, feeding, bathing, and sitting. We pass a pool inhabited by a small multitude of terns, those black-capped birds that fly upwind beak agape and screaming, and that every fisherman knows as the mackerel gull. We watch half a dozen who, with wings flailing and water flying, are giving themselves and each other a violent salt-water bath.

But wait! What are those birds on the bank there above the pool? They have no black caps. Their heads are gray. Of the size of oversized pigeons, they have pearl-gray wings and snow-white breasts. Now I have the glasses on them while my companion thumbs the pages of Peterson's *Field Guide*. One takes to the air in short flight and the trailing edge of the wings betrays a flashing pattern of white against gray. Then another shows a black band at the tips of its outstretched tail feathers—possibly a young one, this. And they all have a curious black spot back of the eye. I call to my companion—What are they?

Identification complete. Bonaparte's gull—*Larus phila-delphia*.

We pass on after other game. Nearer the shore is a mussel bed, and here we watch the beetlehead plover whose pepper and salt coloration makes an astonishing blend with the mussel shells. Small ring-necked plover soar by in doubles and triples and quickly land. As we approach nearer the bed a greater telltale—a winter yellowleg—gives its shrill warning whistle—*Wheu—Wheu—Wheu*. And here we are lucky in identifying a long stilt-legged wader with a needlelike beak —Wilson's phalarope—a pattern of perfect black and white marking. This fellow is an infrequent migrant on the Atlantic coast.

Up Little River on the west shore of Scarborough Marsh there once towered a grove of matchless white pine. So tall and stately were they that to walk beneath them was to pass along the nave of an arboreal cathedral. Always a soft soughing told of the passage of air high in their tops. You could not see the sky and the light reflected in from the sides was always dimmed. There was no brush, and underfoot, bedded down by the shedding of countless seasons, the ground was elastic with brown pine needles.

This spot, this Eagle's Nest, called for pilgrimages. Often over the years I went there, inevitably. And from the ineradicable tablets of the memory there would be evoked poignant pictures—of that brace of woodcock I flushed there early one spring—of the winter when the snow had the blue tinge of the deep woods—of the kingfisher who always chattered past in curving flight up and down the green creek —of the sunsets watched in reverse with the slanting shadows of those towering pines trending out over the golden grass of the marsh.

Ancient white pine of unknown age, they were the ones in colonial times that bore the King's broad arrow and made masts for the ships that humbled Bonaparte. Of these noble and beautiful trees, four foot and more through at the butt, there were upon my last visit but the butts and tops, cast aside as worthless slash.

It was a sight to break a man's heart.

The bay was like a jewel. Early in the day of a lapis-lazuli blue, in the afternoon of an emerald green, at night it was black jade across which the moon traced a broad path of light. It lay clasped within the curving arms of two long capes. After nightfall the lights scattered along the encircling shores gave to this great gem a setting. And between the capes there rose out of the sea the dark low mass of a double island. Here a single house broke the rounding skyline.

Any day in the month of July, Saco Bay might—and then again it might not—be alive with schools of tinker mackerel. On this score no oldtimer would ever hazard an unqualified guess. Sure, the mackerel would always run. But where? Ah, that was another question. One year the cove beyond Prouts Neck to the east'ard would be alive with them and the year following nary a one could be caught there. Tall tales these oldtimers would tell of "jiggin'" when the mackerel were running strong, of how they ground "chum" for bait and strewed it alongside to "toll" the fish to the surface. And when a school rose there ensued the excitement of their voracious leaping until the surface was no longer water but the flashing white and blue-green bodies of the tinker mackerel. These yarns were never complete without some prodigious estimate of how quickly the old liar had filled his barrel —"jiggin' 'em with nawthin' but the bare hook."

But the night of nights was the night when the mackerel would come ashore. Always there was a moon, round and orange, out of the sea beyond Prouts Neck. Always the tide would be ebbing just as the moon's light would begin to pale and silver. Then somehow in the miraculous manner of the waterfront the word would pass. Men, women, and children came to the beach on the run, laden with every receptacle known to man—boxes, barrels, crates, kegs, baskets, traps, nets, firkins, and their bare hands. At low tide a bar made out, forming a pool. At half-tide this was deep but it steadily dropped as it was drained by the falling tide. Over the bar into this pool the dogfish would be driving the tinker mackerel. You could see their white bellies in the curves of the waves.

Into the swift-running outlet of this pool I would plunge, basket in hand. There I straddled it and stood for a minute, perhaps two, with the basket under water and the fish slithering past my bare legs. Then I would lift out as many as a small boy could tug—my basket filled to overflowing with gleaming silver and black tinker mackerel.

Then as the tide reached its ebb there came the feast of the gulls—circling, mewing, fighting, squalling—they would settle down among the stranded fish that the tide had left flapping and gasping on the sand. Then the ravenous beaks would plunge into the white bellies and pluck forth the entrails until soon the scattered bodies of the gutted mackerel gave meaning to the politician's lampoon of his opponent— He shines and stinks like rotten mackerel by moonlight.

Just what is a tinker mackerel? The learned Mr. Webster tells us it is a young one, eight to nine inches long and probably two years old. This last may be doubted, though we do not pretend to any expertise in the field of ichthyology. But what about a chicken lobster, a spring chicken, a summer yellowleg, or a snapper blue? Are they not all the young of the year, their first season out, as it were, and hence of a distinguished tenderness and singular succulence?

But to get on to the cooking. After they are caught, the next step is to clean them, pausing as you slit that white belly from vent to throat to admire their regularly striped sides so like those high wisps of cirrus that some oldtimer, now unknown, called a mackerel sky. Just as Henry Thoreau did, when passing through a Boston Market, he noted in his journal: "Saw a mackerel in the market. The upper half of its sides is mottled blue and white like the mackerel sky as stated January 19th, 1859."

If by this time your fire is not burned down to a braize, it ought to be. Braize?—a bed of red-hot coals of yellow birch and rock maple from the flat surface of which a myriad tiny blue flames flicker steadily. Now you have your split tinkers in a greased broiler. Sear 'em quickly, first one side, then the other, with a flick of the salt shaker as they are turned.

What's the spider for? Why, tomatoes of course. In they go sputtering in the hot bacon fat. And say, son, set that coffee pot in handy to the fire, will you? She's got to come to her second boil. And have that eggshell handy for settling purposes. What's that contraption? —Why, Mister, that there's a Yankee baker. That's the only fit rig there is for outdoor cooking. Can't have broiled tinkers without blueberry muffins, can you? Ease it up to the braize, will you, so that those muffins will brown in good style.

And so it goes until you sit down and are ready to follow your hand. There it is—a mess of tinkers broiled just to that turn where the flesh still retains and gives off the essence of their sweet moisture, a couple of fried tomatoes, a brown rounding blueberry muffin, and a mug of hot mocha and java.

Hey! Reach there into the wangan—grub box—will you, and fetch out that lemon.

A prime favorite with small boys, duck hunters who want their game rare, and those whose delight it is to traverse the length of lonely beaches is the beach plum. In the early spring of the year the solitary sojourner on the dunes will note with joy their flowering. Those are the days of color on the beaches. The thick clusters of pure white blossoms almost hiding the scattered clumps of gnarled bushes are like whitened canopies dotting the dunes. They gleam in sharp contrast to the brilliant blue, red, and purple blossoms set off by the fresh green of the beach pea and the beach grass. Then the solitary walker retreats to the dunes from his walk by the sea, to stand before this scene of rare beauty.

With the forming of the fruit there arrives the heyday of the small boy. Green, hard, and small, of about the contour of a good-sized marble, the beach plum is then in demand for ammunition in many a pitched battle. Then with the ripening in early September picking parties are to be seen scattered over the dunes. Had Henry Thoreau ever gone after beach plums, he never in all this world would have laid claim to fame as captain of a huckleberry party. Huckleberries indeed! A beach plum party affords the best berrying in the world. Why? Because they are so everlastingly bountifully plentiful. Of a deep purple covered with a lush blue bloom when fully ripe, they hang from the bushes in brilliant hues of blue, red, orange and green, and they fairly rain into your pail as you stand with the bushes breast high all about you, picking steadily in all directions.

Next comes the bustle and the hurly-burly in the kitchen

—the boiling cauldron, the skimming, the corpulent jelly bags festooning from hooks in the beams and dripping endlessly throughout the night. And the next day the long rows of glasses stand in the rays of the sun and reflect a translucent light that is of the essence of redness.

But the pay-off comes in the fall of the year. The two-tined fork is poised above the fragrant carcass of that miracle of the marshes—a hybrid black duck whose mother was a mallard. It plunges in. Swiftly the red juice runs. Deftly the breast is laid bare. Then the duck hunter who likes his game rare may savor it at its best with a generous portion of that tartly sweet beach plum jelly. This medicine is most highly recommended by the oldest practitioners to be served at frequent intervals throughout the winter until the spring of the year when the ducks fly north and the white blossoms of the beach plums are again in bloom on the dunes.

The Maine woods comprise the upper watersheds of four large rivers—the Androscoggin, the Kennebec, the Penobscot, and the St. John, which latter includes the Allagash and the Aroostook. These waters drain numberless lakes, ponds, and bogs, tracing out an intricate pattern of streams and thoroughfares. They weave their way past ridges and around hills and mountains, all timbered. Ktaadn lies within the yoke formed by the East Branch and the West Branch of the Penobscot. Any bound that separates these waterways is known to those who travel these woods as a height o' land. This may mean a few rods or as many miles, and they form the numberless portages that link this great primitive system of transportation, perhaps the oldest in use in the nation.

Thus a man so minded may still travel the length and the breadth of these woods in a canoe as did the Jesuits and their Indian allies in the French and Indian Wars; as did Benedict Arnold in his march on Quebec; as did Thoreau whose memorable excursions in the years 1846, 1853, and 1857 are of record in *The Maine Woods;* and as have hosts of men before and since—Indians, trappers, woodsmen, surveyors, timber cruisers, river drivers, lumbermen, game wardens, guides, and sportsmen. Nowadays this is fast disappearing and in another few years it will all be a thing of the past for the bulldozers are cutting roads through these woods at a fearful pace.

As we paddle along that stretch of the Moose River below Attean Lake that forms the thoroughfare between Big Wood Pond and Long Pond, and then ride through the little rip under the bridge at Jackman, we are greeted by the kingfisher. He dives from his perch on an overhanging alder and sweeps in a long swooping flight around the next bend. This is to show us on our way, for when we round it there he is again, poised on the dead branch of a birch stub, very important in white collar and dark blue cockade. And now again he is off downstream sounding his *cr-a-a-a-a-ck* like a watchman's rattle and thus heralding our approach. Indeed the kingfisher is both guide and guardian of these deadwater stretches of the Moose River.

Then we come upon the lilies! Amid patches of green there are single ones that in the distance look like cups filled with white petals on green saucers; and again amid shades and shades of flat green leaves rimmed by the dark water, there are clusters of them. We stop to pluck one and I bury my nose in its evocative fragrance. Delicate and haunting and nostalgic is the odor of this white and gold wide-open lily.

In a concentric pattern four green petals opened first, to be succeeded by a circle of nine petals of a slight pink that is turning to white, then another white-petaled circlet of nine, and finally a ring of seven. At the heart of this cluster of white petals is a mound of solid yellow gold from which arises, again in a circle, a tangled pattern of golden tongues. Seventeen of these have orange tips and there are countless yellow tongues small and large.

Thus does this small sun face the great one that has caused it to open this summer morning. I insert the long stem in the gunwale and let the end trail overside that the blossom will retain as long as may be, its freshness on the bow of the canoe. Then we gather the yellow lilies that some call spatterdock. They are like golden lover's knots atop of long green stems, and soon these line the opposite gunwale.

Thus decorated our argosy proceeds upon its appointed course. And as we slip out from beside the alders where we have been gathering our lilies, the kingfisher again takes off, this time flying so close, as he winds up his rattle, that the red of his waistcoat can be seen under his black and blue jacket with its white flashings.

Then we wind down round the bends of the Moose River into Long Pond.

This day in response to a "Nice mornin'," I hear one say: "Yes *sir!* Air's jest like wine, ain't it? A man could walk a mile on eggs an' never crack a one."

The timbered hillsides that run in easy decline to the water's edge are flecked with patches of shadow that are cast upon the treetops by the slow-moving clouds as we cross Attean Lake and enter its upper pocket. We are headed, my companion and I, for a chain of ponds and by midmorning we have traversed the first height o' land and paddled across Clearwater Pond—a deep dark eye in the midst of the forest. Here is a short carry, on which the upturned canoe, like some ponderous animal, weaves slowly through the underbrush on the shoulders of my companion. This leads us into Benjamin, the next in the chain.

This is a considerable body of water bounded by a curious combination of bog and ledge. In the bogs the low thick sedge is broken by tapering hackmatacks whereas the ledges support a stubborn growth of scrub pine and in some places they descend bare and sheer into the water. Here we dispute possession with a wild loon.

Have you ever heard a loon cry? Some say that they laugh and the figure of a laughing loon is indeed a common figure of speech. Yet, albeit this cry is often shrill and wavering, it is not the laugh that marks them in the mind's eye of my memory.

I put my glasses on this one. She is swimming between a couple of islands with two young ones in tow. I see her powerful mandibles go agape and vibrate. And there rolls forth that long, mournful, eerie, haunting cry, to sweep across the surface of the water, assault the ledges, reverberate in the aisles of the woods, and at length come echoing back from the ridges. This true call of the loon has a yodeling effect between the rise and fall of inflection, and it is the wildest of wild sounds.

Then I hear it again—this time from the stern of the canoe. It is my companion calling. This is an art that I lost in my boyhood. With the fingers of the right hand clustered and clasped between the left thumb and index finger, you blow sharply between the knuckles of the thumbs, and there issues forth a low, moaning cry remarkably akin to that of the loon and to which it will respond readily. The yodeling effect is produced by the rise and fall of the two smaller fingers of the left hand.

"Wait now, I'll cross her up."

This time the call comes forth without the broken yodel. This is even more mournful and haunting than before. For a considerable spell the loon is silent. Then she responds in kind.

For an hour we sit here thus, on the surface of Benjamin, calling the loon and listening to the rolling, haunting echoes of her weird wild cries—*oh-ooo-la*.

In the afternoon when we carry over the height o' land into Horseshoe, the last pond in the chain, we encounter another old acquaintance—the white-throated sparrow. He is so close indeed, that I can reach out and touch him.

On any April morning in the wake of an early shower when Bringhurst Woods are amethystine in color with the sun shining through the clearing mist, they will ring and ring and ring again with the sweetly quavering calls of this white-throated sparrow—*all day fiddlin'—fiddlin'—fiddlin'*. And then after a bit he is heard no more.

In midsummer, if you are lucky enough to have followed his trail to one of his favorite breeding grounds in the north of Maine, you will encounter him again. Perhaps on a carry as you pause at the top of the height o' land to shift the weight of the outboard motor you are lugging, again as you float on the winding deadwater on the other side of the carry between alder-lined banks that hide the bogland on either side, his call will come to ear again—*old Sam Peabody-Peabody-Peabody.* You whistle your reply—it is easily done— and then after a pause from some dark thicket hidden deep in the woods, he will give answer, again and again, for as long as you want to pause and converse with him before passing on your way.

With our lunch on the shore of Benjamin over and a thundershower threatening, we hurriedly paddle to the portage, make the short carry, with the bottom of the canoe again weaving through the trees like the back of some strange animal, and reach the little camp around the bend of Horseshoe just as the rain is commencing to fall. In one of the camps where we sit out the shower, the sides are open breast high, and within touch balsam and spruce rise to the height of the roof.

Here, within arm's length, flitting quickly in and out of the thick spruce sprouts is the whitethroat. I watch him closely and at ease without a glass and am surprised to see how vivid are the yellow spots between the beak and the eye, and what a spruced-up appearance those uniform black and white streaks give to his sleek head. And then, of course, there is that telltale triangular white patch at his throat.

At the height of the downpour he disappears, he and his song, so that the silence is given over to the drumming tattoo of the rain on the roof. But when, in a dozen minutes, the sun is again glimmering through to make the raindrops on the spruces sparkle like amethysts and the shower can be seen and heard retreating over the next ridge to the eastward, he comes flitting and flicking about again. There must be a nest hard by. I wonder if they are ever found.

The experts—the ornithologists and their kin—have given him a very fancy name, *Zonotrichia albicollis,* but up here where he breeds he is known simply as the whitethroat, and the common phrase heard on every hand is:

"Did you hear that whitethroat this morning?"

"You fellers made up your mind what you're goin' to do today?"

Then without waiting for an answer: "Tell you what you do. You take right out round the corner of the island and you head for that highest mountain over there in the east. Keep your eye peeled on the shore, and when you see them alders open up, that there's the mouth of the Moose River. You can't miss it, possibly. You run right up to the first falls, and then you backtrack 'bout two hundred yards, and you'll see a little brook comin' in there through the alders on the right-hand shore. And . . ."

The barrage of fast spoken directions continues, to end with: "And keep your eyes open. This time of the year you're goin' to see bear, deer, moose—most anything in there."

Here we are at the mouth of his brook, a mere trickle down through the alders. The canoe secured, we clamber with some labor up the clay bank. For a bit there is a ridge thick with hemlock and fir. What was that? A low clucking. Then a *whirr* of wings—once—twice—and a brace of young partridge have flushed to sit in foolish ease within easy gunshot on the branches of a hemlock. The hen, mewing, stalks in sedate dignity back over the ridge. And so for a moment we watch the playing out of the ancient game—the enticement of the enemy and the protection of the brood.

Then after we traverse the height o' land come more alders. In short order they open up and we come out into a logan. The word "logan," a corruption of the Algonquian word "pokeloken," is met on every hand in the north of Maine. Connoting primarily a pocket or inlet in the course of a stream, it is indiscriminately used to designate any low marshy place—in this instance an open boglike place where a small body of water has been backed up by an ancient beaver dam. Here in the deep thick grass is the shining bottom of an overturned canoe. Over she goes and in we get to paddle up to the head of the flowage where another beaver dam, smaller and newer, backs up a pool. Here for a bit we wet our lines but catch nothing but hungry mosquitoes.

On the way back it happens. This little pond doubles in an angle and we are emerging from the far pocket. At the turn where the breeze ruffles the surface I see two black heads swimming toward us. Beaver? The paddles stop and the heads continue to come on. Then another black head breaks the surface and another and another. They are up wind and they neither smell nor see nor hear us. Diving and rising, they are like the heads of small boys at play in a swimming hole. Now they are less than ten feet off.

The two foremost rise up out of the water to a height of a foot or eighteen inches—sleek black heads, long necks, and bewhiskered snouts. A series of short sharp little barks resound:

Char-char-char. Char-char-char.

Otter—five fat otter!

Of a sudden they dive and the water hides them.

Didn't the fellow tell us we would see "most anything" in here?

The next day's excursion takes us in to Number Five Bog. The derivation of this curious place name is this. The unorganized township just south of the northerly line of the historic Bingham Purchase, which forms the southerly boundary of Attean Township, goes on the maps by the name of Township Number Five in Range Number Seven. Its population is zero. In the local nomenclature all of its physical aspects bear the identifying phrase—Number Five. Thus there is Number Five Mountain, the tallest west of Kataadn, and at its foot on the opposite side of the Moose River lie Number Five Field and Number Five Bog.

"You folks plan to go in there this mornin'? It's quite a sight, I tell you now. I'll tell you folks just how to go. You can't make it possibly."

In following our informant's complicated directions, we get involved in a confusion of *two* white birch woodpiles by the side of the tote road, and for a time we are lost. At length there comes a yell from deep in the woods where my companion has gone cruising. The intelligence is that he has located a yard—an ancient clearing for storing logs—and in I plunge. Then suddenly I catch sight of the old teakettle hanging in the birch that marks the start of the trail. We follow the ancient spots down over the side of the ridge and come out into a patch of muskeg. A knoll dark with pine and spruce lies before us and after we traverse it, there before us lies Number Five Bog.

A wild, a desolate, lonely place where the scattered hackmatack struggles to the height of a man and dies. A place of pitcher plants—they are in bloom—and rare flowers and deep moss that later will be a glory of color. The abode of the black duck, the moose, the deer, and in years past, of the caribou. In this great saucer of sedge, cupped between wooded ridges and lofty hillsides, for the space that we are here we are unspeakably remote in a vast silence.

Stretching endlessly the wet sphagnum lies in every direction. Here and there it is peopled by the stunted trunks of dead and dried hackmatacks and by the sparsely needled branches of those that still struggle to survive. At the far-distant edges of this wide-open space in the midst of the Maine woods, it is rimmed by a line of dark spruce. Then at an even greater distance there slowly rise the hardwood ridges, then the hills, and finally the timbered mountains that cup this scene of desolate beauty. In the southwest the wooded escarpment and the bare bald top of Number Five Mountain tower aloft and there the fire warden's lookout rises like a thin clean needle in the clear air.

The walking is as on a vast wet sponge. When I jump the surface shakes, and with each slow step that I take I slump through the clinging moss into the water. There is a sudden loud swish of wings overhead. A loon, seeing us, has suddenly veered to crash land, as they do, out there on the surface of the big bog pond. At this juncture a distant muttering roar comes to ear, and aloft up there in the upper blue is the passage of a four-motored plane. What a contrast between these two worlds!

With a song sparrow celebrating the event we launch our rubber boat and row laboriously to the point, a curious geologic fault in the middle of this vast bog. It consists of a knoll of fast land, covered with conifers and bordered by considerable boulders. Here we go ashore and celebrate our successful passage by a cooling and refreshing swim in the dark reddish water of the bog pond. Here also we take our nooning. It is pleasantly cool, and the place is filled with a vast silence that permits of the hearing of small noises that are ordinarily missed. There is, for instance, a high whining, a sort of keening, that comes from a myriad of flies high up amid the spruces. We watch the slow scaling of a marsh hawk on an endless reconnaissance out over the bog. Now and again he turns upon tilted wing but he never comes to rest upon any perch.

After lunch there is time for a small excursion around the knoll whereupon the immense stretch of the bog becomes even more apparent, extending as it does in flat expanse in all directions away from this slight wooded eminence on the shore of the pond. There are no paths, only game trails, and these we follow, exploring a little logan that makes in on one side of the pond. I chip a profusion of gum from the dead stub of a spruce.

And the flowers. All through the bog pitcher plants thrust up through the reddish brown moss. I chance upon some rare wild flowers—three wild orchids. There is one with a spike of pale and lovely white blossoms, beautifully clustered. This is the white fringed orchis. Then growing in the shade of a clump of sheep laurel on a long stalk are the purple blossoms of grass pink. Finally, as the sun is falling toward the skyline of the surrounding hills and I am slogging wearily through the wet moss toward the rim of the bog, I come upon a small pink flower of singular beauty and a faint fragrance. This turns out to be rose pogonia by some called snake-mouth.

All this I learn later from the books when I lay my specimens down beside them for identification.

For me, a huckleberry party is one of those nostalgic adventures evocative of a barefoot boyhood, scratched legs, mosquitoes, and those luscious blue and black berries that drummed on the bottom of my tin pail and then mounted and mounted until at last they were flush with the brim. And then came the long walk home in the twilight with the pleasure of consumption yet to come.

Give me a stone-strewn mountain top where the huckleberries and blueberries grow in equal profusion. Or then again burnt-land, where they multiply in even greater profusion. In some quarters, it is said, they burn over the ground in the fall of each year—great stretches of it that are known as the blueberry barrens.

What is the difference between a huckleberry and a blueberry? The botanical gulf is no doubt of consequence, but of this I know nothing. Their difference in the field is manifest. Your huckleberry is of a dark black hue, is ordinarily of a uniform size, which the blueberry is not, and it lacks the bloom that characterizes the cerulean blue of the blueberry. In addition there is the taste, each unique and all I can say is that the blueberry has a blueberry taste, the huckleberry tastes like a huckleberry and their combination is ambrosial. Then there is a distinction between the low bush and the high bush betokened by these terms and chiefly of interest to the berry picker.

It was on a clear cool August day that I crossed Attean Lake, found an old trail through the growth of popple—poplar—and birch that had succeeded to the pine forest burned over a generation ago, and clambered up the side of the mountain called Sally Mountain on account of some legendary female who once got lost on the top and spent the night out. Halfway up I got a cooling drink at a spring where I had a long close sight of a yellow-bellied sapsucker, and at length came out suddenly into the clear to look upon a scene of memorable beauty. The lake at the foot of the mountain strewn with pine-clad islands, great stretches of green woodland rolling between ridge and hillside and broken by the blue of some inaccessible pond or the yellow of bog, and a horizon of hills and mountains, bold and sharply clear of contour, this Maine landscape was a view for remembrance.

Here were the blueberries and huckleberries for which I had come, gleaming blue beneath a blue sky out of patches of green that grew in the crevices of gray granite. I had but to sit and pick and pick—then hitch my seat along to the next patch and start picking again.

Twenty-four hours later and several hundred miles distant, a considered consultation attended the production of my two-quart pail of blueberries and huckleberries. Old recipes were cited and idea competed with idea on how best to prepare them. And then at the end of dinner, by common consent, there appeared at the head of the table a great round deep dish surmounted by a crisp brown crust on which here and there stains of dark blue juice betrayed its content and inner succulence—a deep-dish and by some called a deep-sea—blueberry pie.

What a feast that was and the fittest conclusion for a huckleberry party.

The Fall
of the Year

In the late afternoon of this early September day there is abroad an air of tense expectancy. All day long it has been warm, humid, even sultry. A haze has hung about the sun. The wind, veering now in one quarter, now in another, has been an affair of fits and starts. With portents such as these the oldtimers, having cast squinting glances aloft, dust their knees with their beards and mutter to each other of weather breeders and a "no'the-east storm." And from Eastport to Hatteras the storm warnings are flying.

After a dull and sullen sundown there comes the start. It is a gentle rain, easy and soft-falling. Then as darkness gathers, the wind gathers. I see the swish of wet-leaved branches against the panes and hear the splatter of fast-falling rain. Sudden gusts shake the frame of the old hotel as the wind mounts its fury. And when I turn in at midnight to be lulled to sleep by the rising storm outside, I know that in the morning towering seas will be rushing ashore.

For my vantage point in watching the surf I stand upon the dunes hard by a rocky point. Aloft, low in a louring sky, the scud rushes overhead out to sea. Over my left shoulder comes the wind, steady, strong, and in occasional powerful gusts. The tide is making and in toward me rush the seas, hurtling ashore in an unbelievable turbulence and with a vast elemental roaring. Slowly my ear, accustoming to the booming roar, catches varied notes in this symphony of the sea.

Near at hand is a sharp rasp as a wave sweeping up over the hard-packed sand and surging past the tide line reaches, before it is spent, the foot of the dunes. Then with its receding there comes the prickling of a myriad tiny air pockets bursting from the suddenly inundated soft sand. Beyond and above the level of these nearer notes is the ceaseless rumbling of tumbling surf on the successive plateaus of white water rushing shoreward. Overtopping all is a steady booming as the crest of an oncoming comber curls in a forward leap, breaks, and then falls.

From the point come the intermittent pounding concussions of heavy water plunging down upon exposed ledges and its sharp smack against the side of a rock as a column of white spume plunges aloft, mingling with the sucking sounds of the seas receding from the rock weed. In back of the dunes all these separate noises merge in the great roaring I heard at first, and up ashore this becomes muted, waxing and waning in inexplicable change. This, in the colorful phrase of the Maine coast brought down by word of mouth from the west country fishermen of sixteenth century England, is the rote—the rote of the sea.

On either hand in distant coves plumes of gray spray, torn by the gale from the crests of the waves racing toward the sands, are like the manes of sea horses galloping shoreward. Through binoculars I watch off Seal Rock the lustrous emerald green in the curve of a wave making up to crash in whitened fury upon that distant ledge. Viewed from an angle

I catch the volute of this wave in the moment of its curving and see how, in the breaking of its whitening crest, it over-leaps the wave to enclose a roll of air before booming down to leap aloft again in spouting creaming foam.

Directly out in front is a welter of white foam where lies The Old Proprietor. There, a mile and more distant, the seething turbulence of the sea, when seen through the glasses, moves, with an almost stately dignity. Masses of the white water in columns and clouds surge and are tossed aloft to be torn to spray by the gale, and then to subside into the path of an oncoming comber that erupts in still an-other and ever variant white spectacle. Here is the unbeliev-able beauty of the surf that once caught the eyes of Winslow Homer and lives forever fixed by his imaginative insight in his imperishable marines. Within a couple of miles to the westward of where I stand, in his studio on Prouts Neck, year after year, he watched and watched and painted and painted this endless mystery of wind and waves and sea.

I shift my stance to the point to the east'ard, and from here above the level of the sea the binoculars reveal secrets of the surf that are hidden from the naked eyes—the drops of gray spray shredded clear by the gale, bits of rock and rock weed flung aloft clear of the white surge of the surf, and the black slats from a wrecked lobster pot thrust above the surface in the white cresting of a wave. I am not alone in my watching. A sweep of the glass reveals single figures and groups dotting the rocks on the Cape Shore, at Prouts Neck, and along the beaches. Scattered among the rusticators, as all summer visitors were once called along the coast of Maine, stand lean-visaged men who watch from beneath long-visored fog-cutters, and women with shawls drawn over their heads—natives, people with salt in their blood—called forth from their homes by the never-ending mystery and the compulsive beauty of this no'the-east storm. It is always so termed by the true-born down-Easter.

In the next cove the stone-strewn shore is alive with shore birds running, teetering, and feeding upon the wealth of microcosmic life cast up by the seas. Here and there and now and again a plover flutters up into short flight. With a sudden surge of unexpended vitality the flattened crest of a wave sweeps up over their feeding ground. In startled sequence they peel off the shore to mount, to wheel out over the surf and to flare, a swift flying constellation against the gray spray. The glasses reveal the flashing black and white pattern of the ruddy turnstone, the solemn black vestment of the beetle-head plover, and the pure white of the collar of the ringneck. The now spent sea recedes. In they curve, their tiny whistling cries piercing the rote of the sea, to land and busy themselves with their feeding again.

This is the moment of the squall. The corner of my eye catches it steadily blotting from sight the skyline of pine on the next headland. In the next instant its cold slanting rain strikes the back of my neck and sends a shiver of expectation down my spine. It sweeps swiftly out over the sea and all is now blurred. The seething of the seas breaking over The Old Proprietor, the contours of the islands and capes alive with leaping surf and the white cresting of the seas—all this is now seen indistinctly through what oldtimers term the "drisk." A cold penetrating rain this, and it drives me, soaked and shivering, to seek shelter up ashore.

But midafternoon proves the squall to have been the clearing shower. Now the louring scud lies leaden against the horizon to the south'ard. Overhead clouds still move seaward in steady procession but here and there they part to let through slivers of pure blue. The wind is dropping and soon the sun will pour down on the magnificent seas that are still rushing and tumbling ashore. Then across this swiftly shifting scene, lighted here and there by the slanting rays of the sun, there move out to sea in widely separated quarters of the horizon three distinct squalls. These moving curtains of rainfall are like great gray palls let down from the sky. The edge of one of them sprinkles the beach. With the sun breaking through upon this apocalyptic scene, it is like one evoked by the terse entries in an ancient log—Heavy seas—variable— squalls. So ends this day.

Come nightfall the beach is deeply dark. Few stars are out. Again the tide is making and the rote of the sea is rising. Far out from shore a wave breaks, creaming white in the darkness. I count four levels of white water gleaming in the murk, as successive waves make their way toward the beach to rasp and to die upon the sands. Beyond The Old Proprietor with the rise and fall of the seas, there flick on and flick off the lights of a coastwise vessel, her green light bespeaking her westerly course along the coast toward Boston. The no'the-easter is blowing herself out to sea. And by dawn she is gone, lost in the wastes of the Atlantic.

For sheer delight in mere being give me a September day when the warming sun has burned off the chill of early morning, when the air is crystal clear, so clear that where sky meets sea there is a long taut line above which projects a white stack with its black plume of smoke and the masts of a distant freighter bound unseen toward an unseen destination. On such a morning, as the sun approaches the zenith, there will come a moment of time when there will dance upon the entire surface of the turquoise-blue bay golden fillets of reflected sunlight. This is a moment and but a moment, to be caught and treasured in remembrance, for with the swift turning of the sphere such a vast reflection of glancing sunlight is only a passing phenomenon. In that instant the great mirror that is the sea has been angled precisely right for my contemplation.

In this setting stands The Old Proprietor. On the old charts—circa 1835—this ledge bears the legend "Seen at low water." The accuracy of this early warning to mariners I can attest, having on this same morning seen its two outcroppings standing out of the placid sea as I walked across the flat beach at low tide for an early morning plunge into the sea. And this *was* an ebb tide. The bones of The Old Proprietor were bare, bleaching in the sun and for once almost dry.

Half tide is the great moment in the life of The Old Proprietor. Particularly is this the case on the day after a no'theeaster for then a heavy sea will be running. Two combined combers roll and curve up into great volutes in back of the ledge. They tower above it and then, precisely at the middle point, the great crest creams in orgiastic fury and the white surf pours forth, running out on the wings of the wave. Through the glasses I can see great shreds of spray torn from those breaking crests by a wind of gale force. Then in the next instant there is only a tumbling mass of white water and foam.

There are other moments in the daily round of The Old Proprietor. Through a squall of rain he gleams dully and fitfully. At night—on a dark night—his gleaming is spectral white, a dramatic flash in the darkness. Even when the tide is full and he is no longer awash, he still has a warning for the unwary. There is that occasional wave, the ninth some say, that will roll, crest, and break, leaving a swift glimpse of white foam and green. This then disappears from sight as the wave rolls on toward me where I watch from the distant shore.

The Old Proprietor has his visitors. There is the lobsterman who runs his chunky boat, so it seems at this distance, almost upon the ledge. There he idles his motor, hauls his pots, and fills his well with lobsters. A fellow by the name of W. Snow, as I deduce from the red and white buoy that I cut loose from the trap washed up ashore on this memorable September morning, and now have as a memento.

In the moonlight The Old Proprietor puts on a particularly spectacular show. On a day when the wind in the afternoon comes brawling out of the southwest, rolling white caps from the waves and smoking—a smoky sou'wester, they call it—at sundown a circle of haze will line the horizon. And then when the moon rises it mounts like an orange orb on a pall of darkened haze.

The deserted beach curves into a long sweeping crescent of sand. In back the dark plumes of the pines shoulder into the sky where the stars hang in a blue-black canopy. Out in front lies the vague mass of the unlit island and from time to time a breaking of white betrays a distant ledge. Then there is the sea. It is calm now, almost placid, yet in endless motion giving rise to a ceaseless crescendo. There is the crashing of the wave, then the muted rumble of its oncoming surf, the small sucking of its last fling up over the sand, and finally the spent sweep of receding water, repeated without cessation.

Beach and sea are bathed by a half light in which familiar things are cognizable yet obscure. The shadows that it casts are vague and there is no clean-cut line between light and shade. It is this quality, I think, that gives to moonlight its peculiar dreamlike quality. As the waves roll shoreward and their slopes and low troughs are broken by smaller waves, the light of the moon plays out in reflection a dance of golden lights that flash and then fail and then flash again in a never-ending pattern.

The Old Proprietor lies in the far distance. Later with the rise of the tide the ledge is no longer awash, and the sudden flashes of white that ordinarily betray the breaking there of the distant wave no longer gleam. Instead the wave that rolls above the ledge fixes with its multiple facets the reflected golden light of the moon. And in the distance it is as if there floated for a moment on the surface of the sea a tumbling of golden coins. Then they sink. For several moments the sea is dark. Then another comber erupted into a roll by the bones of The Old Proprietor once again covers the surface with those glittering golden doubloons.

For a long time I sit and watch this scene in silence, listening to the endless rote of the sea and counting out my good fortune in the golden coin of the moonlight and of the sea.

At sunup a man may walk this beach utterly alone and hidden from the world by the long low dunes and the waving beach grass. On these early fall mornings there is a nip that goes with the smell of fresh salt air. The sand underfoot has been swept clean and clear by last night's tide, and I stride along secure in the thought that these are virgin sands on which the line of my tracks lengthening out behind me is the only sign of man. The sea is calm, and to the clear fine line of the horizon, of a deep, deep blue.

Ahead, the beach is flecked with flashes of pure white against the deep brown. There a colony of gulls stands and feeds amid the kelp cast up by the recent storm. A sudden whiff, strong and putrescent, betrays the presence of a dead seal. Now the gulls are getting up, the larger ones ambling awkwardly over the sand before their widespread pinions render them air-borne. The air is filled with them—flapping, rising, soaring, skimming overhead, and screaming all the while that strange inimitable cacophony that characterizes the flying gull with beak agape.

Then, striding through the kelp, I come upon the reason for this large congregation. Scattered in profusion amid the seaweed are quantities of large hen clams. Generally they lie deep in the sand beneath the sea but when an early fall storm coincides with spring tides, they are churned to the surface and rolled ashore in the surf. This is an opportunity not to be missed. Off comes my shirt and on it in jig time a small mountain piles up. Swinging the load over my shoulder I turn and retrace my steps, this time into the sun. And all the way back my mind runs ahead to evening when I will slide my knees up under the mahogany to the most savory and succulent dish known alongshore—a tureen of steaming clam chowder.

To sit on these dunes with my knees cocked up to support a well-focused pair of field glasses is a richly rewarding experience. In this wise I bring myself into intimate contact with the life that teems on the foreshore—that broad expanse that lies between the means of high and low water and is purged each day by the tides in their eternal rhythm. The best time for watching is when the tide is making.

I see perhaps the rolling fins of three porpoises who always travel in schools. Now their brown pointed backs roll above the surface, visible for an instant, and then still rolling they disappear, to reappear a few seconds later on the crest of the next comber. Or again I may glimpse the bald black rounding dome of a seal when its head emerges and its eyes gaze shoreward with a curious expression of vacuous incuriosity. Then it submerges as innocuously as it had appeared to pursue its hidden course. This apparition may well be the cause of the rippling of the surface by a school of small fish.

This in turn summons the terns, and they fly in, bills agape and screaming. Theirs is a cry that is wild, unmistakable, and indescribable. I pick one out and follow his flight. Upwind he beats, his black-capped head twisting, now to this side, now to that, his black beady eyes alert. Then, with wings set, he sweeps downwind past me in a swift curve. Of a sudden a wing tips up. He turns to fall like a plummet and splash into the trough of a wave. Then wings beating and dripping he climbs aloft with the head and tail of a sand eel curving from his beak.

Some twenty feet in the air an extraordinary thing happens. With a flick of his head backward the eel is tossed aloft and then caught again in its descent. I lower my glasses. Can they belie the facts? I would have said so but for the fact that a few seconds later I watch a repetition of this phenomenon. From the swallow that follows the backward flick I surmise that this is to line up the sand eel for consumption.

In the surf there are coots. Great black and brown sea ducks, these are the scoters—white-winged, surf, and American—of the bird manuals. In a disordered flock they swim into the sharp northwest wind just beyond the break of the waves. Now and again one will come in too close and, as the curve of the wave rears, I catch a printlike glimpse of him with his head and back above water and his breast and webbed feet visible paddling furiously in the green water. Wait! That one missed his trick altogether and is tumbling end over end in the surf.

Then there are the small shore birds—peep, ring-neck, and

sand pipers—endlessly running, first away from the wash of a wave and then in pursuit of its recession, their black legs twinkling, until of a sudden they rise in a living cloud to sweep out over the foaming surf, and wheeling, alight farther down the beach to pursue their feeding there amid the seaweed.

When the tide is at its lowest ebb the scene is different. Off the point to the east'ard small waves break lazily on the outer ledge. Where the beach merges with the rocks, there makes out from the point a mussel bed that is flecked here and there with small pools left by the receding tide. As I walk on it, I penetrate the rich and faintly putrescent odor that tells of the presence of shellfish long exposed to the rays of the sun. Beyond lie rocks and ledges crowned with deep masses of brown rock weed that slip and squelch underfoot, and after the sea runs in they glisten with sparkling drops of salt water.

His head—and that remarkable bill—are the first I see of him. In a delicate curve downward this long bill runs forth from a small head, the sleekness of which is pronounced by perfectly aligned and sharply clear streaks of black and brown. Stepping gingerly on his stiltlike legs, he emerges from behind the rocks. Of a delicate buff color with letter-perfect mottled markings, he stands in clear relief against the dark brown of the rock weed. There is no mistaking this fellow—the Hudsonian curlew, *Numenius phoepus hudsonicus*. But wait—there's another one. Good Lord, this fellow is nearly twice as big. He is the size of a large spring chicken or a hen pheasant. And that downcurving sickle-shaped bill of his must be half a foot long. It may be that this is that rarest of the rare ones—the true sicklebill, *Numenius americanus*.

Now I have flushed them. As they wheel and flare in swift

flashing flight out over the water, the air resounds with their clear high-pitched calls. The big fellow with his long scimitar of a bill, his neck in a broken curve, and his long legs trailing astern, suggests a miniature blue heron in flight. With the glass I follow them into the next cove where they alight to feed on another rock weed pasture.

A half century ago when I was paddling barefoot on these sands, Jack Curlew was a truly rare migrant in the early fall of the year. In the gun rooms along the coast the occasional report of a glimpse of him always caused some oldtimer to withdraw his pipe from his mouth and spin a yarn of the good old days when gunning was really gunning.

"Why, mister, they wuz as common as peeps, I'm tellin' yer."

Then for many a year Jack was not seen at all in these parts and folks thought he had gone for good. But today, thanks to the sound conservation policies embedded in the Migratory Bird Treaty and its accompanying legislation, they are coming back, and you and you and all of you may now see Jack Curlew with his long curved bill on his semiannual excursions to marsh and beach all along the coast.

Taking its rise in the Province of Quebec, the Moose River winds in a long and perpetually curving course between ridges, past bogs, around hills and mountains, and through thoroughfares that link an extended chain of lakes and ponds until after emerging from Brassua Lake it pours on down into Moosehead Lake opposite Kineo Mountain. While encircling but before entering Attean Lake, its course makes a great oxbow.

Here above Attean Falls it winds ahead through bog country. Each stretch is a length of deadwater where the current is imperceptible. The banks are high and grown thick with alders. Beyond there rises the tall spruce, tapering aloft, and the larch, or hackmatack as it is called, rears its scraggly form against the sky. Here an occasional elm spreads its wine-cup beauty, giving a strange domestic touch to the wild scene. Farther still where the ridges rise there is hardwood and the forest spotted with the black of pine and fir.

As we paddle slowly up this placid stream the ever-present kingfisher sounds his sharp rattle and launches himself from the dead stub of a birch to fly before us in a long flight bending toward the water. From bend to bend in flight after flight he ushers us on our way. A muskrat swims parallel to the course of the canoe. I can see his sharp snout cutting the surface, the long lines of the cut-water widening behind him, and, as we overtake him, the brown back depressed below the surface. There is a sudden flip and a splash as he dives from sight. So now I watch a bittern standing poised at the edge of the stream, secure in the illusion that he is not seen. His streaked brown and gray body stands out against the clay bank—he should have chosen the long sedge for his background—and his long neck and bill point in a straight line skyward. So he stands utterly motionless. Never in such a stance have I seen one move. And so we pass on our way.

Suddenly out in front a great blue heron is in flight. I had not seen him, so perfectly blended was he with the bar from which he had arisen. The great wings rise and fall once, and then he glides on, dropping slowly toward the water. Then again they flap once, the tips kissing the surface, and he sweeps on on extended wings. His flight is an alternate succession of flappings and glidings. Now he is disappearing far ahead on slowly undulating wings. The alders at the next bend obscure him and we travel on.

Then around the bend we put him up again. This time I spot him first, and I take note that he literally leaps up into flight, crouching before he leaps. Then, as he is air-borne, he gives a couple of auxiliary thrusts with his long legs before folding and stretching them out in a long line behind him. This time he does not follow the thread of the stream but soars and rises over the height o' land that makes the next bend in the stream.

We paddle steadily on. Again he is in flight. This time he is flying downstream, his long bill shifting from side to side as he surveys the course of his flight. On and on he comes, closer and closer, and I note the orange-yellow splotches that mark the outer joints of his wings. His long neck curves down toward his great body, then up again, and he is like some strange craft in flight.

He sees the canoe—flares awkwardly—flaps once—and then soars on set wings up over the shore of the stream, to be hidden for a moment by the wide spread of a spruce, before sinking behind us to settle and to stalk undisturbed on long legs in the cove where we had first seen him.

It is late in the afternoon when we catch up with him

again. We are back-tracking, going downstream on our way back to camp on Birch Island in Attean Lake, when by good chance the canoe pokes its nose around the alders without disturbing him. There he is standing at the head of a bar on a mass of driftwood. For a bit we watch him stalking and feeding. Such a meticulous, such a dignified striding this is, as first one long leg slowly withdraws out of the water, clenches its toes and then swings a couple of feet ahead, to be followed in like measured manner by the other. With his long bill extending down over his chest and occasionally swinging from side to side as he glances sharply here and there along the length of it, he has the aspect of some very wise hunched-over old man.

Suddenly his long bill shoots forth with force and precision into the long weeds by the shore. Then aloft I glimpse the disappearing feet of a frog. An ejaculation from the stern of the canoe startles him and, crouching, he leaps aloft. This time there rises a roar from the outboard as we speed in hot pursuit. With his great sweeps pumping ponderously he mounts until he is traveling at the height of the trees. But he seems to be having trouble—that half-swallowed frog no doubt.

Then all of a sudden and when we are abreast of him, he seems to halt in midair, the great wings beating, and his long legs drop down. They clutch the topmost tip of a tall spruce. It cannot hold him but bends this way and that. But there he stays, his pinions outstretched and beating the air for balance.

It is an extraordinary sight—as if some great antediluvian bird had caught up with his talons and was attempting to fly away with the sphere.

In camp in Umbazookskus Meadow—so runs my old journal entry.

This was at the foot of the stream of that name where it enters the waters of Chesuncook Lake—by some called Suncook. The next morning a poled ascent would take our party to Mud Pond Carry, which in turn would lead us over the height o' land into the famed Allagash waters. The term "meadow" derives from the earlier days of lumbering when the winding shores of Umbazookskus Stream had been bordered with long rich woodland meadow grass, a pasture deep in the forest, where annually there would be gathered the hay for the horses and oxen used in the winter lumbering and on the spring drive.

Today this campground lies in deep water—"flowed out" in the vernacular of northern Maine by the raising of the level of Chesuncook Lake by Rip—Ripogenus—Dam. On the night that I camped there those meadows had long since disappeared for the same cause and in their stead there towered on all sides of this deep dark tarn a forest of gaunt gray stubs, the trunks and limbs of dead timber. Again in the vernacular this is known as "dri-ki"—the dead trees killed by the backed-up flowage.

On the opposite shore to the eastward through the dri-ki, the dark blue sky was paling, heralding the rise of the moon. The occasional *terr-r-r-r-rump* of a bullfrog broke upon the silence to be answered on another shore by the same note in a different key. Seizing his axe the Frenchman clipped a couple of billets from an old pine stump and tossed them into the braize. A shower of sparks ascended into the dark air and the flames curled around their dry edges.

Through the naked dri-ki there now shone the topmost golden sliver of the moon. And as it slowly ascended a pale light poured through the dri-ki into the tarnlike pool. Long shadows formed. The bullfrogs ceased their tromping, leaving the deep silence to the low sputter and hiss of the small fire. For a few passing moments the great golden moon outlined the dri-ki in a chiaroscuro that gave to the scene the sombre aspect of Gustave Dore's tortured trees in his depiction of Dante's Inferno.

Ya-a-a-a-nk!

A sudden shriek of sheer terror shattered the stillness. Then came another and then another. They punctuated a steady splashing and thrashing and thumping. Then, as suddenly, the cries weakened and waned, and then died away altogether. The moon, now clear of the dri-ki, filled the dark silent pool with pale light.

It was the Frenchman who broke the spell.

"Das a crane in de cove. Mister mink, he see heem when he stan' dere in de moonlight. Dey suck dere blood, you know."

In the morning before leaving Umbazookskus Meadow we paddled over into the logan. Some scattered feathers there were and lying in the shallow water amid the weeds, the bedraggled body of a great blue heron, the mute and soon to be disintegrated evidence of this woodland tragedy.

Old Jake's last name sounded like McCarran but the way he spelled it, it was MacEarhan. As Scotch-Irish as they make them, he was an ancient product of Prince Edward Island—a "P.I." in the inexplicable usage of northern Maine and the Provinces. I learned that Jake was a P.I. in the following fashion.

We were in camp up on Smith Brook, the guide and I, on the carry halfway between Eagle and Haymock. Haymock is a lake to dream about. Away off the beaten track it is, in the watershed of the Allagash—a dark round liquid eye in the depth of the forest, cupped and surrounded by hardwood ridges and rimmed by the darker outline of tapering spruce. We wanted to go back there and camp. At least I wanted to, desperately. But we did not do so.

It was mid-October. The skies were louring. And so we considered and debated over the dry bacon, the steaming coffee, and the great smoking slabs of golden johnnycake; and as we did, those heavy clouds began to sprinkle. By the time breakfast was over, the sprinkle had become a pouring rain soaking the forest and dripping relentlessly from the trees. This did it.

"Le's go see Old Jake."

Suddenly the vision of his tight little cabin, secure from wind and rain, a hot supper, and a dry bunk where I could listen to the tattoo of the rain drumming on the cedar shingles became infinitely alluring. We broke camp, toted the canoe and the stores and gear to the foot of the carry and set out.

A long hard drag it was to the deadwater, barelegged in that cold water and on those sharp stones, then endlessly paddling around never-ending turns between banks of low sedge dotted with bedraggled hackmatacks, until finally after hauling the canoe up ashore to dump the rainwater out of her, we set out across Eagle Lake in search of the thoroughfare leading to Chamberlain. We paddled in an incredible downpour so thick at times as to obscure the shores. At long last the dripping logs of the old dam came in sight and there in the clearing stood as neat a little cabin as ever met the eye of a woodsman, with a tapering column of gray smoke mounting into the rain-laden sky.

An hour or so later came the episode that was revelatory of Jake's origin. Through the chinks of the stove I could see the red of flame, from the black tin stovepipe there came the tinkle of the cinders as they rushed aloft, and throughout the one-room cabin I felt in puffs the welcome heat of the stove. This was causing steam to arise from my clothing and the ease of dryness and warmth to surge up inside me.

Jake has made some biscuits and now he stands at one side of his double-ended oven, ready to slip in the second batch. There is a deft twitch with a moccasined foot, the door clangs open, and Jake shoves in his pan, alas a bit too far. The other door swings wide and out tumbles the first pan. His biscuits with their rounded brown tops cascade and scatter all over the floor. Old Jake surveys the wreckage:

"Well," says he, "ye'll always know a P.I. by the size of his chips."

By contemporary standards Old Jake was an oldtimer for he dated from the days when only long lumber was driven on the Penobscot and when, in the American imagination, the river driver stood high in the ranks of his peers—the cowboy, the mountain man, the keelboat man, the blue-water man and the Forty-Niner. This wiry sawed-off splint of a man with watery blue eyes that must have taken color in his early days from the light glancing off the Bay of Chaleur was a superb woodsman. With naught but the common tools of his trade—his axe, saw, drawshave, and a crooked knife—Old Jake had fashioned with his own hands his cabin here deep in the woods. Log dovetailed with log, from the ground to the eaves, the timbers, the flooring, and the finishing, all hand tooled, and the roof of split cedar slabs combined in a compact ensemble against the dark forest.

The next day I took a picture of Old Jake sitting on the high porch of his cabin. While the result does not, as he had evidently anticipated, appear in his picture, I have a most pleasing recollection of his preparation for his portrait. From up under the eaves he fetched down an old cigar box and rummaged around for quite a space in the assorted debris of nails, screws, chalk, cartridges, and what not. Finally he dredged up and adjusted in his shirt band over his bulging Adam's apple—a collar button.

A perfectionist, that is what Old Jake was.

But much as this handiwork of his was admired, it was not his cabin that brought forth the gleam of achievement in those old pale blue eyes. Down at the other dam which held these Allagash waters from pouring down into the East Branch of the Penobscot and which was also in his charge, he had built himself an outhouse—"a regular carker" in his own words. And as we took our departure he made me promise to visit it, whispering the secret spot where lay hidden the key.

In due course when we ran down past the arm of Chamberlain to the foot of Telos Lake, I paid a visit to this native American antique. It was worth the trip. A path over well-stubbed roots led me by twists and turns through the trees into a small declivity. There amid the shadows of the spruces she stood. The carefully peeled hemlock logs gleamed spectral white in the shade. A neat semicircle of whitewashed stones invited the visitor to the door. Inside was paintwork—the walls in pastel green, the covers a sky blue, the seats of warm inviting brick red. But it was only when the door was closed that there was discovered Old Jake's true genius. For there before my eyes as I sat, neatly lettered and neatly tacked at the appropriate height was a sign—Old Jake's request addressed to the casual sojourner:

PLEASE BE AS NEAT AS A CAT IS.

Always a tale goes with this. Old Jake's camp at the Chamberlain Dam was one of the showpieces on the Allagash trip, and he had many visitors.

"One day they was a party come through here," he told me that night. "Funniest rig I ever seed. Jes' two women an' a clergyman. No guide ner nuthin'. I jes' couldn't figger it out. Well, I was showin' 'em round an' we was comin' back from the spring. This clergyman, he nudges me, an' then he says, kind of whisperin'-like:

"Mister, kin the ladies use your privy?"

"Mister," I ses, "I'd ruther they did."

The Country of Delaware

Hour upon hour in the fall of the year I have sat in a blind on Thousand Acre Marsh in a perfect contentment of mind and body. Out in front is a cut, perhaps seventy-five yards wide, traversing the marsh on the bias. This, so I have heard, is the forgotten bed of the St. Georges River before it was diverted into the course of the Chesapeake and Delaware Canal. Here there swim into the wind in a carefully calculated pattern the decoys.

In every direction an eye-stretching vista carries my eyes in a restful and contemplative observation. At the rim of the marsh beyond the stretch of marsh grass, the upland mounts in easy contour to merge at the skyline in a field of tasseled corn, or to trace out the familiar shapes of a group of farm buildings, or a copse of wood shouldering irregularly into the sky. This is the rule save to the east'ard where runs the causeway, from whence there comes occasionally the distant hum of a motor, and where in the faintness that precedes the dawn or in the dusk of twilight, a long beam of white light proclaims the swift passage of a car. Beyond lie a stretch of salt marsh and then the river. Here at sunup I have seen a half of the great red disc hold in black silhouette above the level of the marsh the booms, the stacks, and the superstructure of a passing freighter.

As I sit alone, the middle of Thousand Acre Marsh is the remote center of the universe. Overhead from low horizon to low horizon is the great vault that is the sky. Here is the backdrop for the presentation of an ever-shifting scene— a sky that is cloudless, air that is balmy, and a complete lack of wind—a bluebird day in the gunner's parlance; or a sky filled with a turbulence of swift flying scud, spitting down upon the marsh, snow, and sleet that stings my face. Then there is the mystery of the paling promise of the false dawn, and at the end of a long afternoon the glory of the afterglow. These are the sights I go to see. And I never tire of watching.

Oddments of experience come to mind as I write. A muskrat in a long traverse of the cut, his wake widening behind him until it stretches from shore to shore. Then the sight of him sunning on the rounded dome of his cattailed house hard by. The hawks that sail over the marsh endlessly soaring on fixed wings that tilt with their turning. The blackbirds, a living constellation, making of the marsh with their incessant chattering a sociable neighborhood. A fish hawk clutching a carp that to all intent flies in the same direction as its captor. An occasional flight of swans in a stately traverse, the air echoing with their high soft *coo coo coo*. Geese in flight with their clangorous resounding. Crows in distant flight forever cawing. The belching, welching, watery sound of the hidden bittern. A marsh wren in the feather grass that I could have caught in my hand. And duck—the whisper of their unseen wings, the soft calls, the high flight etched against the cirrus, and the taut tension that comes when they turn to my call and pitch to my decoys.

Of all this am I a part when I sit in the blind alone out on Thousand Acre Marsh.

In the dim light a low level of dark cloud lies barely visible along the eastern horizon. In that quarter it is black and, out there beyond the causeway and over the salt marsh and river, murky. This is the retreating scud of yesterday's rainstorm. Overhead the heavens are clear and of a deep dark blue. The stars are steady points of light in the cool clear air. A small wind whispers through the reeds by my ear, and a spray of grass decked with drops of rain bathes my cheek as I turn. From afar and from all directions the faint gabble of water-fowl betrays the ducks hidden in the millet busy at their feeding.

A beam of white light travels north along the causeway, and there is the distant hum of the motor in the still air. A cluster of red and white lights that by some magical process is drifting slowly westward bespeaks the passage of a freighter through the Chesapeake and Delaware Canal. Astern of her the lift of the Reedy Point Bridge is in slow descent.

There is no false dawn. Yesterday's cloud bank obscures it. Gradually the marsh lightens and a gray replaces the blue of the canopy overhead. Then in the west long fingers of cloud stretch aloft. This is good—the sure harbinger of wind—and in our blinds we gunners rejoice as the whisper of un-seen wings comes down from aloft. Those clouds on the western horizon stretch and grow and reach aloft and even over into the eastern sky. Soon all the marsh is overcast and dull save for a slot of blue above the scud in the east where the sky is still clear.

Then of a sudden the rays of the sun, still hidden behind that low-lying bank of scud, strike against the clouds that have progressed out of the west. In that instant—and it is an immortal instant—Thousand Acre Marsh comes on to blaze with a warm golden light. This gives an illumined meaning to the old familiar phrase of the Odyssey—the rosy-fingered dawn. It is as if from a myriad hidden pyres an effulgence of golden flame is rising everywhere. Never have I seen marsh grass gleam so yellow, nor the open water so deep a blue and the next instant a path of shining steel. Aloft the colors of the clouds form and fade in evanescent shades of purple, of olive, and of pearly tinted gray. Against the canopy of cloud the waterfowl are etched in black as they weave and reweave their patterns of flight, circling and turning before this kaleidoscope of shifting colors.

The rise of the sun this day is one for remembrance and its setting is no less remarkable.

A great orb of red in the gray haze on the horizon—this is the sun at the moment of sundown. Suddenly it sinks from sight, and for a moment the marsh is bleak and cheerless. I shiver a little. Then the hidden rays slanting aloft to the zenith bathe the wisps of cirrus with warm tones. Here yellow merges with olive, olive with purple, and purple with pink. As I plod out across the marsh to the causeway, this phase of the afterglow wanes, the clouds seem to dissolve, and with their disappearance the sky begins to take on the depth of darkness.

Yet the afterglow continues. At the rim of the western horizon lies a long curve of fiery red. Once I am on the causeway I take note of a phenomenon. All afternoon out of the northwest a steady breeze had been rippling the open water in the marsh. This breeze has held and the dark waters still dance to its tune. But only in the open. For where the grass grows, the water is still and the surface calm. Here the afterglow is reflected from the zenith in a hundred pools of molten gold and red where the millet and the marsh grass grow in dark abundance.

Then the waterfowl, whose massed flight from the marsh I had watched in the last hour of daylight passing high over the blind, begin to return. Singles, doubles, and triples flash swiftly overhead. Aloft larger flights fly in high. Many disappear into the dusk out over the marsh. Others set their wings and scale down or, settling almost vertically, plash into some pool of molten gold amid the millet's dark sprays. In the quiet of the evening I become aware of the noises of the night taking over—the low welcoming *quack*, the soft *kuta-kuta-kut—kuta-kuta-kut* of the black duck's feeding call, the *frawnk* of a crane in some hidden cove. The day is done and all gunning is over. Once again Thousand Acre Marsh is a safe haven amid the millet for the mallard, the black duck, the sprig, and the little green-winged teal.

Far and away the most dramatic talisman of the fall of the year is the swamp maple. This is the beacon that in the late days of August stands by the New England roadside and proclaims in scarlet panoply, to a world that is still green, the coming change in the season.

"I was startled," recounted Henry Thoreau in September, 1853, while descending the West Branch of the Penobscot River in a birch-bark canoe, "by seeing what I thought was an Indian encampment, covered with a red flag, and exclaimed 'Camp' to my comrades. I was slow to discover that it was a red maple changed by the frost."

The best vantage point to experience the fall of the year is in the deep woods. Find yourself an old pine stump or a log and sit quietly for a space. Then perhaps, as once happened to me, there will come pattering on the dry leaves a red fox to drop his haunch and sit surveying you, as leaf after leaf after leaf detaches itself and floats silently earthward.

Or perhaps late on some Indian summer afternoon after traversing the hardwood ridges in search of grouse, you will chance upon in a hollow amid a thick growth of pine and hemlock, a single swamp maple rising aloft. The effect is magical and of extraordinary beauty. Through the crimson foliage the slanting rays of the setting sun strike a glowing effulgence of rare pink light that descends and is reflected like an aura beneath the tree. In a few moments it will fade swiftly as dusk comes on.

Once many years ago in New Brunswick I saw across a swift-falling stream, a swamp maple in full leaf, the color of deep blood red. The night had been cold, freezing in fact. And as the smoke from the campfire mounted, a chilling wind came sweeping upstream just after dawn, bearing in its course a flurry of snow. I stood and watched the icy fingers of this north wind tear at the crimson leaves. They fell in clouds and were blown hither and thither. Soon the shore beneath the tree, turning white with the slanting snow, was flecked with red hearts. While I watched, this maple was swept clean of its foliage until its gray branches whipped bare in the wind. It was winter that was at hand.

And so in my mind the phrase, the fall of the year, derives directly from the annual phenomenon of falling leaves. In a word, the fall is the time of falling leaves.

Upon stepping outside these October mornings the air is sharp, chilled by the heavy frost of the night before. Throughout the quiet Bringhurst Woods a leaf here and a leaf there detaches itself and falls slowly in a series of little fluttering sideslips. Each falling is an event of note and finality.

Beneath a Japanese maple there lies a patterned carpet of crimson and black where the cinders of the roadway are strewn and in large part obscured by the starlike leaves that have fallen during the night. This glowing red carpet is the toll exacted by the frost. Three leaves come to rest on the fender of the car and I examine them. Each has seven sharp points. In the slanted sunlight of early morning they glow against a background of light blue. Then I notice that they are scattered in profusion amid the deep green leaves of the holly that stands next to the maple. This is a phenomenon of note. It is exactly as if the holly had been spangled with natural Christmas decorations.

I look about for more. The stately ginkgo stands at the edge of the lawn with upraised arms, still a mass of gamboge. Yet here again the green grass is completely hidden by a gleaming yellow carpet composed of a myriad of curious fan-shaped leaves. And hard by beneath the drooping mulberry, the tapestry is of a pastel shade of olive yellow.

Back in the woods and out of sight above the tops of the still partly leaved oaks, the crows are gathering in caucus. Their incessant calling is a reminder that I must get on my way and be about my business. Yet I stand here bemused with these circular patterns of glowing color spread upon the ground by the first frost. For such a scene as this is of evanescent beauty. Only in the slanted early sunlight are they glowing and effulgent, these singular carpets of yellow, olive green, and crimson spotted with black. When the sun is an hour higher they will begin to dry out and their glow will fade. Then they will soon be mere autumnal leaves, to be gathered into piles, to give off great clouds of pungent white smoke, and be consumed.

The fall of the year is not only a time of falling leaves. It is also a time of far-flying birds. Often I am aroused out of a deep sleep these fall nights to become slowly aware of the approaching clangor of migrating geese. In the mind's eye, as I lie awake, I envision the V winging south just over the tops of the oaks. Talking they are, leader to flock, in the discordant clamor that harmonizes so strangely with their passage. Then it commences to fade. They have passed. The night is silent. I drop off again.

In this turning of the year upon its axis there occur unforgettable incidents. There is, for example, the curious performance of the robins and the thrushes in the dogwood that stands over the well by the back door.

There is no wind. The air is completely calm. Yet here and there the branches of the dogwood shake violently. Why? In successive flights bird after bird flies into it, and then a moment later flies out of it. But while it is there, it does not alight, but with its claws grasping a small branch it beats its wings violently. This is the cause of the shaking of the branches.

A few moments later I go outside. Thereupon a dozen thrushes and robins flush in separate tangents from beneath the tree. Then the reason is perfectly clear. Scattered on the carpet of crimson leaves are myriads of rich red berries that have been shaken down and on this harvest the birds are storing up the energy for their next migration, at least insofar as the thrushes are concerned.

This is the time of the year when the usual cold weather routine for the birds is started up again. The various feeding stations are well stocked with seeds and suet. The holder for the latter is a latticelike contrivance that hangs on the trunk of a maple, holding in back of a series of bars the bar of suet that is impregnated with birdseed. In flies a bluejay. He is ravenous. Clutching at the bars, he drives his beak deep into the fat. Then, withdrawing it while he swallows, he wipes it on the bark with a sidewise motion of his head. Then there is another stab into the suet and another and another.

What strikes me is his tail of which I have a perfect view. It is spread fanlike against the trunk of the tree as often is that of a woodpecker, giving to the bird a measure of support. Thereby there is outlined for display the perfect marking of his long tail feathers—the serrated bars of black against the bright blue and the brilliant white of the outer tail feathers. This is a considerable show and it lasts until the bird, surfeited with fat, flies off into a clump of rhododendron, sounding its harsh cry.

The woodpeckers are making their annual stopover. This same day I was witness to a memorable fight between two of them—such a caterwauling and a marvelous exhibition of twisting turning flight. Then there was that interesting sight of three of them backing in parallel lines down the trunk of a tulip poplar. The sapsuckers with that flashing white patch running the length of their wings were much in evidence and the flickers were legion. And I still recall the half hour when I pursued through the glasses the fast flitting yellow spotted rumps of a pair of myrtle warblers amid the thickly needled branches of an Atlas cedar.

As I write, with the sun warming my back and a soft breeze rustling the tinted leaves, there comes to ear, faintly and from afar and sounded but once, the thin, wiry, tinkling, whistling song of the white-throated sparrow—the finest sound, so one has said—in the wilderness.

The fall migration of the grackles in the Delaware River Valley is like a biblical revelation, and in Bringhurst Woods this is an annual occasion. On an early overcast morning in October the green lawns will be spotted black with them. On the way from one unknown port of call to another, they have come in overnight and are busily feeding. Now and again a small black cloud rises into the dogwoods and smaller trees, then descends again. As I drive out to the highway they peel off the ground in front of the car like shore birds put up by the strolling of a solitary walker. A quarter of an hour later when I return not a single grackle is to be seen. Have they gone for good?

At midday with the sun high, it is warm and the woods are very still. Then all of a sudden they, or another horde, are here again, having flown in from heaven only knows where. In and out of a towering beech they flit, their burnished black bodies in startling contrast as they alight on the steel-gray branches amid the golden leaves. The silence is broken, a wild symphony of cheeping chatter taking its place. This goes on for five, perhaps ten minutes. Then they are off again, as suddenly as they came—their small black bodies zooming away into the distant sky in repeated bursts of flight.

Late in the shank of the afternoon a loud and incessant *tchuck-tchucking* pulls me out of doors. There they are again —this time in the tops of the tallest oaks—in droves, their coal-black bodies standing out amid the green of the leaves. They are nervous, with odd ones flitting from one treetop to another. And always the steady chattering—compounded of a thousand squeaks and rasps into a not unmusical strain.

Suddenly this dies away. They are off, peeling off the limbs and out of the treetops into a huge flock that commences circling around the northerly and easterly horizon. In the southerly quarter there shoulders into the sky another line of treetops—oak, copper beech, tulip poplar, beech, and hemlock. Into the leaves there they disappear and settle.

Armed now with the binoculars, I follow. From a distance I can see the ends of the uppermost branches of a beech in unwonted motion as the hungry grackles scramble for their footholds. Bits of shell patter on a tin roof below, and here and there a golden-brown leaf flutters down as they tear at their sustenance. In the field of the glass I fix one—a large handsome bird—in a perfect focus and at the right angle to the light so that the iridescent feathers of his back and shoulder shine and gleam. For a long time the flock feasts, chattering and tchucking. Then again silence falls as they take off and I watch them into the far sky—an elongated flock of small black bodies in bounding flight.

And this time when they go, they all go—of a sudden and for good. The beech is a deserted tree and the world seems a poorer place. A leaf of life has been turned down—in the fall of the year.

On the ridge lining White Clay Creek it is still dark, the eastern sky being but slightly tinged with light. In the quiet cool air, the sense of expectancy that precedes the dawn is heightened by the clarion call poured forth from the swelling throat of some cock of the roost, poised and bursting with his outpouring toward the dawn. A refreshing sound, this, and it is its own reminder that in modern life something vital has been lost to those who never hear that heralding outcry.

Suddenly, quietly in the murk overhead, a flight of duck swings past out over the cornfield we are traversing, then turns, sweeps back out over the bottom land bordering the creek, gaining height, turns again and lines out toward the eastern sky and the broad reaches of the Delaware River. This is ever a breath-taking sight.

Now in the growing light of the false dawn the silo, barn, and outbuildings of a farm show their shadowed forms. In the farmhouse a single window glows. Fields and darkly wooded hillsides are variantly shadowed patches. A great billow of white mist visible above the treetops and winding between the ridges marks the hidden course of White Clay Creek.

As the sunlight streams through the wooded skyline in back of me, I pass down the steep side of the timbered ridge into the sea of mist. White Clay Creek is smoking, the mist rising in steady wisps the length of its rippling course. The brush is thick and soon, plowing through it, I am wet to the waist. A sharp squealing that retreats steadily upstream tells of the hidden flight of a wood duck. Around a bend I flush four mallard out of a pool in a sudden alarum of quacking and beating wings. Then the far shore flattens out into bottom land and I come out into the clear.

The sunlight is blinkingly clear, the sun being about an hour high and shining just above the level of my eyes. Here are scattered hawthorn trees wet with heavy dew presenting their complexity of branch and dagger gleaming black. Through one a growth of honeysuckle provides a deep green backdrop for the round red fruit. Through these I pass and, the stream inspected, I turn about, facing the sun.

By my passage a miracle has been worked. In the brilliant sunlight these hawthorn trees stand transfixed. They are refulgent with flashing rays. Long lines of pearled gossamer run from tree to tree. They are supporting cobwebs that are miracles of pearled perfection. Through round dewdrops the rays of the sun pass translucent flashes of light. By moving my head slightly, I see in a dewdrop here and in one there the successive flashings of cold light. From one angle the blue that lurks in a moonstone flashes at me. From another a shining of ruby red reflects the surface of a red hawthorn berry. Again I incline my head and there is the yellow to be seen in a canary diamond. Before this jeweled tree I stand feasting on these variable flashings of transflected light, and in this brief quarter hour the wealth of the Indies is mine.

When this happened I was traveling westward through a stand of scrub pine, quartering away from the sun so as to keep it from glinting straight in my eyes. It was right thick growth with shreds of dry moss draping from the bare under-branches, and I was breaking brush with every step. Out there in front the setter was snuffling his way this way and that over the thick bed of pine needles that covered the forest floor. Then all of a sudden something fetched me up with a round turn just as if there had been a line around my waist. And there it was a few feet to the right.

As bright a bit of blue there in that shadowed light as ever caught the eye—a blue as full of remembrance as that of a kitten's eye or an old Delft cup. It was as if a bit of the sky had fallen through the top of the pine beneath which it grew. A slender stem with regular leaves at regular intervals and on top of the stem a cluster of five blue blossoms each one shut tight. What was it? Whatever it was, it was rugged for I picked two clusters and wore them all the rest of the afternoon in the lapel of my hunting jacket, and after that from the heart of Kent County to Brandywine Hundred before they saw water. Two days later they showed only the slightest sign of wilt.

The books gave me the answer—*Gentiana Andrewsii*. This classical name traces back, according to Pliny, to the discovery of certain curative properties of this flower by King Gentius of Illyria. But its popular name—the bottle gentian—derives from the fact that the blue blossom, unlike that of its cousin, the fringed gentian, never opens. And this is a pity indeed for within is another lovely hidden flower—a bright yellow tip with tiny green horns arising from a pale green stem, surrounded by white walls streaked with perpendicular lines of deep blue.

Now the thing that sticks with me is how this little cluster of blue blossoms on the forest floor stopped me in my tracks as I was passing it by with something else on my mind. But then I have had that sort of thing happen before as when a cardinal flower signaled to the corner of my eye out of the green with a flash of scarlet flame.

It is still pitch dark when I arrive at the edge of the slight height of land that trends from the south into Thousand Acre Marsh. At the far edge of this wide area of darkness there is strung out from east to west a line of lurid green lights marking the course of the Chesapeake and Delaware Canal, and beyond, the horizon sparkles with the clustered colored lights of the new refinery amid which, blazing against the blackness, is its great torch of yellow flame. Over to the eastward there runs along the skyline a faint streak of gray. Here in the darkness of the marsh it is cool almost to coldness, with a light southerly blowing across it, and almost preternaturally still.

Stepping to the water's edge I drop my pole across the gunwales of the narrow skiff and as its *bumble-rumble* breaks the stillness, I hear the splatter of wings on water and the muffled quacking of a flight of black duck startled out of the small cove to my right. Soon I am creeping out through the millet, the long shallow skiff sliding easily with the successive setting of the pole. A lone wild goose, lost from his companions and honking plaintively, comes on out of the darkness. Apparently the *bong* of the pole against the gunwale has attracted him for he flies directly toward me. Then he sees me and I can see dimly his black bulk flare in the murk. He disappears in the darkness, his bearings lost, and calling continuously for the answer that never comes.

I reach the blind in good season—about three quarters of an hour before sunup. The blind faces east, fronting on an open pond in the midst of the marsh. Here the black blocks, that are the decoys, are swinging idly at their moorings. At the far shore there rise darkly the tall fronds of the feather grass, and atop of this in the open sky that lies beneath the canopy of clouds overhead the eastern sky is paling with the approach of dawn.

Waiting in the stillness and the darkness I watch against the dark scud the wide wavering lines of the flights that are now leaving the marsh for the open river. From the feather grass in back of the blind there comes the awakening chorus of the blackbirds. At first this is a soft series of whispered *tchucks.* And as the light grows in the east this increases until from all about there is a chorus of chattering that is almost deafening in the silence of the still dark marsh.

What was that? A dark flash shooting across the corner of the blind. I reach for the gun. There they are, three of them swimming out there amid the decoys. That's the way it always is with teal. They come in flying low, out of the God knows where, and alight with a small splash before your startled eyes. I rise up. They continue to paddle about unconcerned. So I yell. Up they get, two of them lost against the black background of the feather grass and the third higher and outlined against that fortunate expanse of open sky. A single shot and he tumbles into the pond. Then I settle back and let the gentle southerly bring him to the blind.

Now overhead the underbellies of the louring clouds become tinged with pink, as with the approach of the dawn the hidden sun strikes aloft with its rays. Then of a sudden the golden arm of the sun bursts above the horizon. This is an occasion and the blackbirds celebrate it with silence and a great bursting of flight up out of the feather grass all over the marsh.

Such is the gunner's sunup on Thousand Acre Marsh.

In the afternoon out there in the blue water the decoys tumble to the tune of a west wind. This is a strong wind and steady that is sweeping over the marsh, tossing the tasseled tops of the feather grass into rolling undulation. It whistles through the thick yellowed grass of the blind and the watching gunners are cold.

An occasional single wings over the marsh and by its bouncing erratic flight I mark it down as a teal. Now there are four circling just above the next cut, their wings flashing as they wheel. Mallard! And downwind is borne the soft clack of a distant duck call, for there is a blind in there before some hidden pothole. Ah! Now wings are set and there commences the long swift glide. Then of a sudden one small black form crumples and an instant later there resounds the *beroom* of a distant gun. Then another folds, plummeting straight down into the marsh. Another *beroom*. The remaining two flare high in the air and line out toward the river. Somebody is having luck this afternoon.

Then, save for the wind, the marsh is quiet and still. This wind grows too strong and you know that the ducks will never pitch, even if they do fly, when the decoys are bouncing about like cockleshells. Nor is there any flight save for the occasional single or double, trending far in over the upper marsh.

In front of the blind now, perhaps fifteen feet off the water, is a flight of ten gulls. They face the stiff wind and with an easy undulation of wing appear to be hovering over the water. I pick one out and watch him carefully. With his head shifting quickly from side to side he is surveying the surface and who knows how far below it. I note the small black spot back of the eye, the white wings and the tail edged with black. Then suddenly he turns ever so slightly and, lifting one wing, is caught by the wind to turn about and sweep down-wind in a swift flowing course. There after a bit, he turns to repeat his slow passage upwind, again surveying.

This fellow is an old friend. Just two months ago I watched him and his fellows in profusion resting on that vast sand bar on the western coast of Maine. Now apparently they are nearer home for in the Linnaean classification they bear the name *Larus philadelphia*—Bonaparte's gull.

Later when the sun is hard by the horizon touching the clouds with color, there comes the blackbirds' hour. I see them first in hordes afar out over the distant salt marsh that borders the river. There are great dusky clouds of black specks barreling through the sky—now up—now down—now up again. They look like blackish clouds against the gray expanse of a real cloud. In a few moments' time they are all over Thousand Acre Marsh. They come in from so many directions that I lose track. Overhead is an absolute canopy of blackbirds. The air is alive with their *tchucks.* A large flock sweeps over the blind and there comes down to ear the sudden soft whistle of their wings.

Theirs is a peculiar flight—a few rapid bursts of wing and then a bouncing coast in an arc of flight, repeated over and over again. Flocks collide and in the collision they merge. Then with a swoop of one end of the flock toward the feather grass, they all pour into it, and that segment of the air is clear of them until, a moment later, they burst out of the grass again in a black cloud of small bodies. Soon the feather grass is full of them, swaying with their weight. Now the marsh takes on a social atmosphere, so distinct does their steadily chattered conversation become.

This evening flight of the blackbirds over a Delaware marsh is one of the great sights of nature. The blackbird, indeed, is one of the most ancient of Delawareans there having been named for him a village, a creek, a marsh and a Hundred.

On the way home this November afternoon the afterglow sharpens the tints of autumn until the red, yellow, copper, brown, and bronzed leaves seem to be tinged by some hidden flame. And afar in the glowing sky great wavering flights of black geese are seeking a safe haven for the approaching night.

A dilapidated automobile is crawling slowly along the causeway. In the distance it proceeds against the vista of the marsh like an awkward insect making a slow and deliberate progress. At length when it draws up alongside where I am sitting on the gunwale of my canoe, enjoying a slab of cold johnnycake and a mug of hot tea, it creaks slowly to a shuddering stop, and the chattering of its valves suddenly ceases. Sunk away down into the worn seat behind the wheel is a leather-visaged individual who wears a long-visored cap of tawny brown and an ancient hunting jacket of dirty brown. Deep-set gray eyes scan me quizzically, taking in my similar accoutrements and appraising the gun that is set against the gunwale beside me. Then comes a query.

How did I do?

This is traditional. It is not, as the phrase to the uninitiated might seem to imply, a form of salutation. This character is not interested in the state of my health. Rather his is a question, an inquiry prompted in friendly interest by one who has sensed in this chance encounter on the sphere, another with an interest as keen as his own. In short his query is directed to the state of my bag, which alas is empty, so I am forced by the circumstances of the chase to respond:

"I did not do good, Mister."

Commiseration ensues, which is then followed in the

normal course of friendly interchange by my query as to how he did:

"Me," comes the response, "I done real good this morning. I jest come off'n my marsh down near Camden. Now I like a marsh a man kin get off'n and on to on a real high tide like this one—no matter how high she runs. I was stuck out a couple of times on a marsh an' I don't want no more of that. Well, I was settin' in my blind an' they was four mallard come up from somewheres away out in front. They're comin' right straight for the blind an' I gets myself all set for 'em. Then one of 'em splits off an' goes to one side. So I lines him up an' drop him—a nice fat greenhead."

In the talking he has suited action to his words, cocking his head to the right, squinting his right eye and stretching his left hand out to support an imaginary gun barrel. As he goes on he shifts in his seat.

"Then I swings right over to the left side of the blind an' down comes drake number two. Then t'was easy, a following shot, to drop one of the hens while number four high-tails it out of there. Four comes in an' one goes out. So I figgers I done real good this mornin' seein' as I got me a teal, a blue-wing too, 'bout ten minutes after the season opened."

He pauses, his saga is over, and for my part I agree that "he done good."

His foot reaches for the starter. The valves start up their noisy chatter, the gears crunch, the tires grate in the gravel, and his ancient vehicle is again in slow motion along the causeway. And as he departs his well-wishing comes to ear:

"S'long, Mister. I sure hope you do good afore the day's out."

In the shank of the afternoon when a November sun is

casting a slanting light across the peninsula, the approach of dusk stirs all the birds into action. Late one afternoon I was at my customary stand at the edge of a soybean field with my back to a copse of brilliantly colored gum trees. Overhead there was a weather-breeding sky—long lines of gray clouds at different heights with the air around the horizon all clear. Beneath the canopy of clouds the falling sun was filling this segment of the sphere with a warm light.

In the grove at my back I could hear the harsh cries of a jay as it chased small birds from their perches. From the trees at the edge of the cripple little flycatchers flew forth in final forays after unseen insects, and now and again a single dove would disappear into the copse. From the marsh that lay in back of the cripple there came the sundown songs of the red-wing blackbirds—their musical *gurgulees* sounding soft in the distance.

Suddenly there flashed in above my head a large flight of doves, a dozen or more in a thick, as it were, covey of flight. They did not see me and take alarm, and for a split second there was a fluttering of wings amid the leaves of a conically shaped gum tree. Then all was quiet and the upper limbs were to be seen decorated with the graceful forms of the doves, breasts and heads high, tails down. It was as if a curtain had gone up upon a perfectly set piece.

With the sunset the waterfowl commenced their trading. High in flight they wove against the sky, their pattern now extending, now contracting. I know one who says that their passage always reminds him of the creeping of the sparks on the dark soot at the back of his fireplace. The comparison is an apt one. Now and again a flight splits in midair into triples, doubles, and singles, and there came down to ear the quavering *quacks* of argument and entreaty.

Suddenly the air was filled with that stirring and indescribable sound, the broken and haunting call of a single wild goose. Directly there followed a strident chorus. In front of me across the soybean field and a road beyond lay a fresh-water pond, and it was there that they were. This meant geese in flight and I scanned the sky.

Far out over Delaware Bay were the specks that were coming and calling. I watched them as they made their long approach while the air resounded with the wild give and take, until on hovering wings up over the pond they settled down out of the air to alight with a great flapping of wings amid a vociferous welcome. Then there was quiet.

In the late twilight as I was about to leave I was witness to a rare spectacle. Quail in flight—not in the single startling bursts of flight that occur when they are flushed—but in a flock, a bevy. They came in unseen, all of a sudden their wings making a small sharp roar. In a flash they passed before me like closely packed hurtling cannon balls in a compact mass. In the instant they were lost to sight amid the trees in the cripple. It was like a sudden apparition.

The flat sands of Sussex County stretch to the skyline in a pattern of tilled fields and open pasture that is intermittently broken by patches of woodland. Here a growth of hardwood, superbly tinted, and there a grove of tapering pine shoulder up into the sky to break into a pleasingly variant contour the monotony of flatness. Scattered and often away back from the highway at the end of a long private lane stand the clustered buildings of the Sussex farms.

As I turn north into the road from Rehoboth the overflowing apple baskets of a roadside stand compel a halt. Here fresh tomatoes—late ripened and the last of the season—are to be had. Fat yellow pumpkins bespeak the approach of Thanksgiving. And, aha!—here is cider, gallon after gallon on tiers in varied tints of yellow to red. The purchases made, there follows a laconic exchange with the close-lipped and leathery-countenanced proprietor of uncertain elderly age upon that topic of perennial interest—the weather.

For there it is in the north and the west—a great wall of black cloud rising from skyline to zenith. On the sides it merges with gray but here in Sussex County it is still clear overhead, and out toward the sea the sky is still blue, tinged with the yellow of fading daylight. Little gusts of wind eddy dust out of the cleared cornfield across the road.

I cannot resist a side trip on a sandy road out to where the marsh begins. Now the wind is roaring. Great swirls of dust rise from the road, trees toss and heave, and across an open field a migrant bush tumbles end over end as if someone were in hot pursuit. A dove soars out of the corn, flares up into the wind, then slides toward the distant woods in a long scaling flight.

Back on the highway the black cloud has now taken over almost the whole of the sky—all save where, out over the sea, a crescent of yellow light is the last reminder of this once blue and gold day. The torrential rain causes a slackened pace, and so I drive on into the thick wet dusk. As I pass Johnny-cake Landing—by some called Frederica—a tinge of yellow, opaque and dull, tells of the disappearance of the hidden sun. Then in a few more miles another crescent of light opens up—this time in the west—opening finally into a broad lake of orange light.

This storm is traversing the Delaware country. Down there in Sussex in back of me all is now black. Here in Kent at Dover the western horizon is still a long lake of dull red gold.

And when I pass over the high span of St. Georges Bridge the great broken tumbled masses of cumuli are scudding downstate, leaving patches of blue-black sky and the gleam of an occasional star. At length, at the end of this day's excursion out in Brandywine Hundred, a half moon pours a cold light on a cold countryside—for now a cold front is moving in, following this storm over Delaware.

The very best way for snow to come is to have it come stealing in at night by surprise—and then to look out upon awakening on a slowly whitening world. At midmorning on this late November day the large flakes are slanting silently earthward. The wind is light, blowing up in sudden sharp gusts that, now and again and here and there, eddy the snow out of its slanting pattern into whirling columns. The northeast sides of the poles and trees bulge with white and the snow gathers and clings heavily to the still leaf-laden branches of the trees. On into the afternoon it snows steadily, remorselessly, silently, and there is no sign of abatement. We are in for a storm, a regular old no'the-easter.

As night falls, the wind rises. Tree after tree after tree shakes out its branches, casting aloft great swirls of powdery snow that drift downwind to obscure all that is familiar in a shroud of white. It is coming off cold. I hug the hearth and the fire, while familiarly to those who live along the seacoast, intermittently and between the blasts of the gale, there comes from afar the warning ominous to all mariners, the foghorn with its harshness muted by the falling snow.

The next day sees the snow still falling, falling, and still it comes and comes until the earth is covered ten inches deep on this late fall day. Then of a sudden it clears and the sun, bursting through, illumines this gift of the gods. All the brilliant hues of autumn—the red and yellow of maple, the wine-colored purple of the pin oak, the light yellow of the birch, the deep rich russet brown of the beech—are like jewels set against the whiteness of this new-fallen snow.

The next snowstorm belonged to winter and it was the event of the Christmas weekend. All the days of the previous week had been fickle and unpredictable. Rain threatened, but no rain fell. It came on overcast, but it burned off. In down-east parlance such days as these are weather breeders. Then came the pay-off on Saturday morning when I again awoke to find the snow moving in. All day long it fell, straight down in slow, silent descent out of a leaden sky, to mantle Bringhurst Woods with a whitening canopy.

Falling snow is almost a mood in itself. Its distinguishing characteristic is a persistent insistence that it be watched. Time and again I caught myself looking out of the window to observe its steady, silent falling. Once, due to an imperfection in one pane of glass, I watched fascinated as the flakes flew upward. Every once in a while I invented a little trip or chore in order to make an inspection outside.

The flakes were large and the snow wet, and with no wind this augured a spectacle. Every branch, each twig, was catching its quota of snow, and all day a steady accretion mounted until the tracery of the trees was outlined thick with snow. In the pin oak a multitude of small spikes of spectral whiteness stood outstretched against the gray sky above its still leaved lower branches, and these latter now and again spilled small avalanches of snow on the ground.

Then by God's good grace it came off cold and so preserved this scene for the next day.

And what a contrast was that next day—brilliant sunlight in the frame of a clear blue sky! To go about my chores in such a setting was an event of a certain privilege. Returning from the woodshed with an armful of logs, the dogwood by the back door came between me and the sun. As I walked toward it, it was transformed into a great cluster of flashing and sparkling lights. There was a constant revelation of new vistas and strange horizons. The thick underbrush and second growth presented a fretted tracery all snow-encased that finally merged with whiteness—but above the top of this, through the snow-laden limbs of the oaks, the clear bright blue of the sky was enhanced. There small clouds like bursts of white cotton bespoke the rise of wind.

In time the wind came and the spoliation of this wintry scene commenced. Bits of frozen snow dropped and shattered on the frozen roadside beside me with ever so slight a crash. The eaves commenced their dripping. Snow sifted from the trees. Yet in the dancing of the branches a myriad of flashing reflections continued to send out special sparkles.

When the unsettled weather of late fall comes to be crystallized by a great mass of cold air out of the north and the west, the rhododendrons perform a curious annual function. Ordinarily their long flat green leaves stand out almost straight from their stems. But on this December night they begin to droop and to shrivel until the whole great clump of them has a stricken, a starving, aspect. This proclaims a temperature below freezing and it is an infallible sign. I have now no need to see how stands the glass.

When they are in such case the gunner knows that his season is doomed. No longer will he go to his favorite marsh. For at Thousand Acre, wherever there be open water, a film of ice is now stretching to thicken with the steady persistence of this freezing weather. No longer does the eye cock aloft to glimpse the far flight of waterfowl etched against the sky. And if the rhododendrons remain in this stricken state, soon the deadwaters of the Brandywine will come alive with flashing figures painting for the mind's eye a skaters' paradise.

There is current another indicium of December. This is the full moon, by some called the beaver moon. The legend is that when the first freeze of December coincides with the fullness of the moon, it is a sign that the beavers are all snugged down in the inner recesses of their houses, secure against the onslaught of the winter that has now commenced.

I step outside of an evening while this moon still hangs high. In its bright light the smooth gray limbs of the maple and the beech are shining, and the effect through Bringhurst Woods is as if a slight white mist lurked there. Then I seek again the open fire where I snug down in the inner recess of my house, as does the beaver. Then I cast my mind back to the long lazy days of summer.

What now of the mosquitoes' hum—the ceaseless cadence of the katydid—the chirrups of the crickets? I remember the rhododendrons towering by the corner of the house and how their leaves, instead of drooping in shriveled aspect, were the deep green background of a great pattern of pink-white blossoms alive with buzzing bees.

But tonight outside it is chill, freezing in fact, and those long tapering green leaves that are my glass now bespeak the departure of autumn, and drooping, have become the harbingers of the blasts of winter.

Winter

The long white beam of the headlights stabs into the darkness without shadow that hangs in Bringhurst Woods as I start upon my first excursion of the new year. The roads are deserted and it is a pleasure to drive swiftly and without interruption through the empty streets of the town, timing my passage neatly to the shifting of the red to the green lights. The occasional traveler I meet abroad at this early hour seems like a friend, or at least an acquaintance, as he responds to the flash of my headlights with a swift winking of his own. Then he is a spot of red light receding swiftly in the rear view mirror, and I wonder what errand it is that brings him forth at so early an hour.

On the DuPont Highway there is the curious small roar of the tires on the grilled iron of the Christina Bridge—I pass a rumbling trailer-truck—then the garish lights of the all-night gas stations sweep by. Across the marsh I mount to the fast land by the old Jacquet home, still outlined in red neon lights as the Kent Manor Inn. The flat length of Delaware with its slight rises and its easy descents lies ahead. It is still dark, and familiar structures are but shadowed hulks in the surrounding darkness. Soon though, the first tint of dawn is in the east and against this dim promise of daylight I glimpse the gaunt stacks, the awkward angles of the towering structures and the round squat tubs of the new refinery that now lies athwart the once picturesque River Road.

Atop of the soaring arch of the span at St. Georges the tinted east presents a long curving crescent of yellow light, and the Delaware country stretches ahead in a flat expanse of deep shadow. Now a farmhouse, a silo, the clumps of shadowed trees silhouette themselves in swift succession against the growing dawn as I pass on my appointed course. This is the time of the false dawn and its pale light is growing. The ice-laden marshes and the frozen flats of the Appoquinimink lie on either hand like great platters of white silver. To the eastward the skyline is now visible—a familiar succession of copses and the regular outline of buildings far from the roadside. Here and there lighted windows tell of an awakening countryside.

At Duck Creek Cross Roads—Smyrna—I turn aside and drive toward the yellow and crimson sky of the dawn. The scattered forms of the dark cedars assume their orderly shapes. Soon now I am headed across a cornfield and then out on a marsh from which there mount quacking the black forms of startled ducks. Then the sun is a fiery ball rising, and for a few short moments the grasses of the marsh and the trees of the cripple that border it are tinged with a strange pale light—a light purple tinge. The geese are now in flight and they fill the air with the clangor of their calling.

This is the first dawn of the new year over Delaware.

This New Year's Day is also a day for skating. Running down the old Dutch Neck Road from St. Georges upon returning from my excursion downstate, I see that the surface of the canal is strewn with chunk ice churned up by passing freighters. Then upon my right hand there lies suddenly revealed in frozen stillness the broad expanse of Thousand Acre Marsh. No flight of waterfowl peppers the sky. No wild cry floats in the cold air. The yellowed feather grass and the millet for once are still. In this below freezing weather the marsh is a painted scene.

In a far cove I see skaters—the widely scattered forms of men, women, and children sweeping in effortless curves, scarves floating behind them—bits of gay color fluttering in the cold air. The ice is thick and burnished like glass. With a bit of wind, what a place and what a chance for a skate sail. This is at noon.

In midafternoon above the dam at Rockland the hidden Brandywine courses beneath four inches of black ice. Here also, between the slopes wooded with bare branches that descend dun-colored to the banks, the frozen surface bears the gliding forms of scattered skaters. Never was there such ice, great stretches of it unmarked—unmarred. Friend meets friend, each startled by the sparkle in the eyes of the other. For this is youth revisited. Never in two decades has there been such a freezing of the Brandywine, so they claim. I can skate from the dam to above Smith's Bridge, in many places sweeping from wooded shore to wooded shore in the broad sweeps that the smooth ice has made possible. The sharpness of contrast recalls to mind that the last time I was on this stretch of the river I was in a canoe, stalking white egrets in a meadow to bring them into the focus of a camera. This is the afternoon.

At night, pursuant to the false promise of a full moon—it turns out to be overcast—this now deserted stretch of the Brandywine is revisited. The yellow flames of a driftwood fire on the ice stab a spot of light in the darkness and of warmth in the chill. Soon there is onion soup boiling and frankfurters broiling and these, with a slight touch of Bourbon, warm the bellies of the chilled skaters.

Then to glide effortlessly out upon the ice, alone into the darkness, and sweep again between the banks that reach in darker shadow up toward a darkened sky, this is an excursion indeed. Then I turn and streak for the warmth and the light of the fire and the cup of companionship.

So ends, near midnight, this New Year's Day.

As in summer, winter too is a season for excursions, and as I head west on Scarborough Beach I am buffeted by a cold north wind blowing off the dunes and out to sea. In the winter months, in consequence of the winter storms, this beach that in summer is a long curving crescent of yellow sand sloping gently from the dunes to the sea now shelves sharply. So steep is its descent that now at half tide, with the sharp wind flattening the incoming waves, there is no surf at all. Instead the sea laps at the sand in little rasps, as if it were the edge of a lake rather than the shore of the sea with nothing but water between it and the shore of Spain.

In consequence of this offshore breeze the air is crystal clear and up ashore the dark plumes of the white pines stand sharp against the sky. Yet in the opposite direction there is a most interesting contrast. In that quarter the rounding dome of Richmond's Island curves against the sky and the blocks of ice and mounds of snow that spot its shores stand forth enlarged. They are of a spectral whiteness, for the island is distorted by a mirage. Curious, that this effect, which is commonly associated with and is caused by the shimmering heat of midsummer, should occur on this raw gray-blue winter day.

The surface of the sea is like a flat floor and I see no motion on it. Then of a sudden, in the middle distance short of the island, a lone coot is in flight. Winding in toward the beach in a long curving flight just above the water, it traces as it lands a long white splash in the dark blue water. Then all is still again. This lone sea bird is the one living thing that I see in this half hour. One other indirect sign of life there is—a small flashing in the far distance tells of the passage of some white-sided lobsterman's boat, but him or it I cannot see.

Up ashore the scene is equally deserted. Scattered along the headland that lies to the east of the beach are houses, squat, square, shuttered, and silent. No light shines. No smoke ascends. No clothing flutters before the north wind. Facing the sea the great windows are boarded over with slabs of yellowed pine. No scene is more desolately lonely than a group of summer cottages closed and boarded up for the winter.

For a few moments I walk at the water's edge with the cold breeze biting my face. When I turn to retrace my steps it is evident that I alone have walked the beach, and I feel a sudden kinship with Crusoe. Then I mount the familiar path that leads up through the dunes, past the securely locked and deserted bathhouses through drifts of snow that are melting slightly, on up past the great barnlike structure of the summer hotel, cold, closed, deserted, and shuttered.

During this short sojourn I have met no living soul, but as I leave I pass the frozen surface of a flooded meadow alive with fast-flying skaters.

That afternoon out at the end of the fish pier and high in the air a gilded cod points its nose due east. Poised steadily on its spindle, it is snuffing, as it were, the wind that now blows from that quarter, chilled by its long journey over the gray waters of the Gulf of Maine. The long edge of the flat roof is lined with the fat forms of white gulls. Were they not alive, occasionally lifting into flight, one would say that they formed a decorative motif, so regularly spaced are they and so still do they stand.

Their flight from this perch is an extraordinary phenomenon. It is always a fascination to watch. Now here, now there, one will half-arch its great wings. Then, while the wings are still in half-fold, so to speak, the steady east wind buoys up that natural airfoil, and the gull is literally lifted into flight, its beak agape and shrieking raucously.

Here is one aspect of the art of flight that man, who even now is etching out a long white vapor trail against the upper sky, has never achieved. To spread a pair of wings and soar aloft on the mere force of the wind—what a sensation, what sport! These gulls do it continuously, reversing the technique and using their sweeping white pinions as brakes as they come down from aloft to settle on the edge of the roof, fold their wings with a nice precision, and stand to survey the scene.

The air is filled with their wild screaming. I watch one waddling on the wet concrete. He stops, opens his beak, and the screams come forth. I note that it is full throated. This is no squeak or squeal, a trick of the tongue or beak. It issues forth out of the very bowels of the bird, and so long as he is sounding his tocsin his beak is at its widest gape and his tail shakes. It is a very vomiting of noise—a broken, hoarse, wild cry that is to the ear what the smell of salt in that east wind is to the nostrils of one who has salt in his blood and his roots deep down on the waterfront.

I watch one astride a high-wheeled cart laden with cod. With his long curved yellow beak he is plucking at a corner of the tarpaulin covering the fish. Now he has a firm hold and, bracing his legs, he tugs and tugs until he pulls back a corner revealing the bare fish. Then the head comes forward, there is a powerful thrust, the beak tears into the entrails of a cod, and now in flight out over the water he bears away a gobbet of gut in his beak. Directly this attracts others. There is among gulls an almost human tendency to profit at each other's expense rather than to make their own livings by the sweat of their beaks. Two of them leap into flight and out after him.

Under attack from above and below he opens his mouth perchance to curse, and the gobbet drops. The gull below snatches it out of the air. Directly the other two are now after *him*. The scene repeats itself, the air flashing with their great black-tipped wings. This time the prize falls into the water. Then the first gull alights and fiercely, with flared wings and gaping beak, defends his retrieved possession. He snaps it up, gulps it down, and the episode is over.

These gulls are an integral part of this waterfront scene. They give it color and tone. Constantly are they rising from the edge of the roof, borne up into the air by the east wind, blowing steady and cold. Never for a moment is the din of their outcries abated. Theirs is a natural and ceaseless chorus. When I look down and no longer see their flight, I still see the sweeping shadows of their scaling passages, passing back and forth over the dock. Also they waddle about, plucking at the castoff heads and tails of the cod. Two will approach the identical tidbit and then, with outspread wings and open beaks, face each other in a snarling fight, whilst a third purloins the spoil.

No one pays them the slightest heed. Men go and come about their work utterly oblivious of the birds flying and shrieking all about them the day long. As they pass, other gulls lazily and with circumspection waddle aside but unless they are cornered they do not fly.

Down in Currituck Sound on the shore of North Carolina low-lying dunes seal off the sea and a dark line of scrub pine marks off the land. Between these distant bounds sweeping from skyline to skyline lies the marsh, traced in intricate pattern by open water in creek and bay. Here on a point, there along the shore or facing some obscure pothole, clumps of yellowed grass betray the blinds. Wherever in front of them, the water is flecked with dark decoys that tumble to wind and wave, there sits the hidden gunner—watching.

The hour of nooning is over. To the eastward where at dawn a saffron sun had suffused cloud and sky with deep dyes of yellow, there is now the leaden overcast of a late winter afternoon. All the marsh colors are muted to blend and fade with the approaching death of the day. Then ever alert in his search for the flight of waterfowl, the gunner's eyes swing aloft to meet at the zenith change so sudden and so sharp as to give to this world of marsh, water, and sky the aspect of an apocalypse.

No longer leaden gray, this half of the sky is blue, a steel blue that descends dark and blackening into the west to merge with shades of deep purple as in a vast spectrum. At the skyline the curtain of cloud has lifted, forming, in the parlance of the locale, an eyebrow—the harbinger of a shift of wind. Here the sun pours forth its molten glow tinging the skyline of the pines with golden fire. The browns of the marshes come alive with the reflected yellow light and the water has the blue of an old Delft tile. A waterfowl winging in lonely flight etches a black passage through the gold of the western sky.

Now comes the wind—in puff after puff after puff, until what at dawn had been a mere cat's-paw creeping out of the southeast, now bowls steady, sharp, and strong out of the creek to the southwest, and comes brawling in over the corner of the blind to set the long blades of marsh grass whispering in the gunner's ear. Out in front the decoys dance to its tune. Then borne high aloft and from afar comes a high wild piping—the sweetly cooing call of the whistling swan.

There they are in the north, those high flashes of white against the steel blue of the upper sky. In ponderous motion the great flock moves south, and as it comes on toward the blind, there takes place the familiar grouping into families of three, four, or five and more. And always the soft muted piping. Almost directly overhead the gunner watches the rhythmic beating of the wings and the ripple of the muscles along the long breasts as these great birds fly with powerfully effortless ease into the eye of the wind.

They make for the bay to the southwest and there against the darkening blue, three gleaming white bodies, wings set, are tracing down in wide circles out of the sky. As they glide below the clear line of the overcast the wings droop and cup, the spiral tightens, and the final descent is made. Just off the water the wide wings spread and undulate twice, like great fans in sweeping motion. They are down. In stately dignity these three great white swans now float on the blue water of the bay.

This is the gunner's remembrance.

Notes from the Gunner's Game Log
Currituck Sound

1949—three days—three guns—six geese, eighteen duck.
1950—three days—three guns—six geese, thirty-two duck.
1951—three days—four guns—five geese, thirty-three duck.

About once in the winter—if we are lucky enough to get a good sharp cold spell, and this year we have had two—the Brandywine freezes over. When it is thick enough for skating you can then get a sense of the stream that transcends any other. Broken as it is by rips, falls, and dams your skating party will have the magic spell of an exploration.

There is that deadwater backed up by the old dam at Breck's Mill. Here, when the skating is good, the ice is dotted with skimming forms as you glide along upstream to pass beneath the soaring arches of the Barley Mill Bridge. Here the ancient domain of the old powder mills commences. The creek bends to the right, forming a rocky wooded island on your left. If you have the patience to take off your skates and walk the shore you are in for a bit of exploration. Soon you come out at the next dam and its deadwater.

The afternoon I was there this stretch of the stream seemed utterly deserted. Yet there was one lone denizen. As I swung out across the unscarred ice, my eye caught, moving in the dusk, along the opposite bank, the startlingly white cheek and jowl of a single wild goose. His body was hidden—there was only that black head and throat with its vivid white patch in swift motion as he got under way. Then he was in the air and on beating wing flew in silence upstream toward the rapids above. On I skated after him.

The open sides of the abandoned powder mills that lined the left bank yawned ominously at me—open, it is said, so that if one in operation blew, it blew right through its one wooden wall out across the creek. Had all of these blown, I wondered?

For a bit I sat on the bank in front of one of these ancient edifices. On the far shore the line of the hill cut a sharp fine line through the towering trees. Here, just visible along the crest the moving beams of cars and, in the distance down-stream, the red and green traffic light at the end of the bridge bespoke the modern world.

Here below on the frozen stream it was different. Here there was dusk deepened by the sharp rising ridges that line each bank; there were the gray granite foundations and walls of a once formidable venture, and a wild goose winging in solitary flight toward some hidden haven in the white water upstream. As I swung swiftly downstream over the ice, the wind blew harsh, sharp and cold. The river was deserted.

I awake to find the world clad in white. Within a matter of moments the snow must have ceased falling, for the sky is still overcast with the light gray-colored bank that is always the certain carrier of snow. In the depth of Bringhurst Woods the whitened branches lace and relace to form a fretwork that in the distance closes together. Higher, the sky can be glimpsed revealing rifts of blue that are widening slowly amid the gray. Over in the eastern quarter there are long streaks where the cloud bank is parting and the edges are fused with the golden light that tells of the approach of the sun. Suddenly a high wind comes down out of the northwest. In its path the snow-laden branches toss and sway, and snow swirls through the air like another snowstorm. Then it passes and the frozen world is still again.

A jay flies into the upper branches of the great spreading beech. Perched on an upper branch outlined against the white snow and gray sky, his crest is particularly prominent. He gives off his sharp harsh cry, a fit note in winter's key, and is joined by his mate. In the distance an unseen crow caws vigorously, also in winter's key. Sweeping swiftly across the sky in the path of a flyway, an airplane passes, dark gray against light gray. In the open doorway the setter stands with poised paw to sniff and to survey this winter scene.

Now the sun surmounts the clouds and its yellow light pours through the widening rift in the cloud bank. The overcast becomes a lighter gray. The blue sky becomes a lighter blue. In the path of the sun the snow on the topmost branches of the old pin oak glitters. Sunlight touches and lights the trunks of the trees. A dogwood that is spread like an expanding globe of white crystals stands apart—an encrusted cluster of snow-laden branches. The dark ell of a house protrudes from the surrounding trees. It is the classic winter scene.

And it seems that this is to last for a while. For the bank of snow-filled cloud has again merged and the sun has been blotted from sight. Only in the western sky does the clear blue remain. And this combination—the white snow on the earth and trees, the gray overcast overhead, the cold blue in the western sky against which the towering trees weave and reweave, one in front of another as they bend before the wind—provides scenes of contrast for feasting and enjoyment long after they shall have passed from sight.

That night when I step outside for a look at the sky before turning in, I notice an unusual aspect of the moonlight on the snow. The moon is almost directly overhead and beneath a wide spreading maple the shadows of the branches lie on the moonlit surface of the snow as if they had been etched there. They are quite unlike the shadows in the daytime. A dainty arabesque of clear-cut lines weaving and reweaving across one another. Beneath the pin oak the effect is the same albeit the pattern is quite different. The clear cold light of the moon hung high in the zenith gives to the snow a brilliance that has a quality of life.

At the edge of Bringhurst Woods there lies recumbent the corpse of an ancient chestnut that died in the famous blight of a generation or so ago. In warmer days than these it is the haunt of a ground hog who likes to sun himself sitting there. But now it is clad in a blanket of pure shining white that in the rising of the recumbent length of the log stands out from the surrounding snow. This and the moonlight give to this monstrous trunk an almost lifelike quality. It is as if a hand were about to stretch forth and cast this blanket aside from the prostrate trunk that would then rear aloft, again to tower toward the stars that glitter palely dimmed by the brilliance of the moon.

All is still—silent as the grave. The trees stand stark and motionless and through them, as far as the eye can reach, the snow shines with the light cast down by the moon. A night of nights this is, only to be seen when there is snow on the ground and a moon hanging high in the sky.

Have you ever watched a full moon trail down the western sky in the pale light of the false dawn? The event is of rare occurrence, though whether it be the result of some magic in the celestial cycle, or whether sloth keeps us abed at the time, I do not know. But this I can affirm. This moonset was an especial event.

No air stirred. No sound of bird or beast or man arose in the morning air. Through the tracery of the trees the sky was gray, a light gray, a uniform gray, that was lightening ever so slowly as dawn approached in the east. In the quiet gray of the western sky, a couple of its widths above the skyline, was the great round moon, a muted yellow orb hung in the surrounding grayness. That was all—the yellow orb, the gray pall, the tracery of the branches. For a few short moments it was like this—without change save for the slow undiscernible descent toward the horizon. This was an experience so unlike the deepening brilliance of the sun at dawn or its dying effulgence at the end of the day as to have an almost apocryphal character.

That full moon against a gray pall hangs high in the memory.

"Snow," wrote Henry Thoreau over a century ago in the wintry month of January, 1856, "is the great betrayer."

After a night of falling snow this is particularly the case with the birds. This morning outside the kitchen window where the birdseed is ordinarily scattered, the snow is all strewn and tamped down by the scratching of small claws. In quite a sizable hole I see the flicking tail of a white-throated sparrow, and now he emerges. Against the white background his markings, which ordinarily blend with his surroundings, are pronounced. The white streaks on each side of his head against the deep brown, the slashings on his wings, the throat patch—all stand out. Then there is the junco and I note the yellow bill and the black cape that fits like a small stole over his head, neck, and shoulders. The delicate colors of the titmouse are enhanced, the pearl gray, the buff on the breast, and the tiny crest—a compact bit of beauty perched on the white snow.

A female cardinal alights, knocking a puff of snow from a small branch of the maple and stands there, teetering with its swaying. The whiteness surrounding her sharply accentuates the minor shadings that are usually eclipsed by the brilliant coloring of the cock. Her orange bill stands out and the olive green that merges with the deeper red gives her a beauty that is the counterpart of her stridently colored mate. Then the flash of crimson that is the cock flies in and stands too amid the whiteness. This cock bird—the coal black that surrounds his polished beak, the sharp crested pompadour, and the flaming scarlet ensemble—he takes your breath away.

But it was the myriad tracks in the snow of which Henry Thoreau took note, and here at the edge of Bringhurst Woods, these are legion. I watch a gray squirrel plunging in small bounds that never carry him quite clear of the deep snow as he betrays his course from tree to tree. Now he is athwart the dogwood that grows by the kitchen door, and his gray tail flicks with more than ordinary excitement. He leaps and dives into the snow, apparently just for the sheer hell of it. For now he leaps up again to cling sidewise to the trunk, and then dives again. The snow flies when he lands and he disappears for a split second beneath it. Then he is off ploughing over the surface to ascend, in a flash of gray, the black trunk of a tulip poplar.

Later, when I get out the car in order to swamp the trail that leads to the outer world, I find that this snowfall has likewise betrayed Homo sapiens. Here in a ditch, there by the side of the road, is the abandoned car—the sluiced team, as it were—snow-covered, cold, desolate, and empty. Those who emerge without chains or snow tires to try their luck on the roads find their carelessness announced to the world— betrayed by the snow.

My friend the down-Easter is still grumbling about being unable to get home that afternoon of the snowstorm. Had to leave his car on the Park Drive, he says, and this kind of hurt his pride. According to his book, we folks in Delaware don't know the first thing about snowstorms and how to handle them. Maybe there is something in what he says. Anyway here is the gist of it.

First of all, you folks never get out with the shovel until it has stopped snowing. Now that's all wrong—like locking the barn door after the horse has been stolen. Why, when I was a little shaver, my old man figured he was late if he wasn't out there to catch the first flake with his shovel. He'd shovel out half the night and finish her off the next morning after the storm had blown itself out to sea. And it paid off too. We never got snowed in. That there is rule number one—you got to start shoveling when it starts snowing.

That goes for traffic too. It goes double as a matter of fact. Now the people in Wilmington have a tough setup the way this town is laid out, stretching between two rivers. Every bridge is a bottleneck. Why, that night I tried to get over three of 'em across the Brandywine. First, there was the Augustine Bridge. Well, it was black with cars creeping in each direction, and on that slight incline leading up from the B. and O. railroad bridge automobiles were slewing around like hot beans on a greased griddle. I says to myself—look, son, this rat race is not for you. So after a bit, and it was quite a long bit too, I weaved my way down to the Monkey Hill Bridge. This was the same dish of tea, only worse. So on I went toward the Market Street Bridge. That was just a morass. They were stuck there in all directions. So I locked her up and left her there on the Park Drive.

Now all that was entirely unnecessary. It could easily have been avoided. All you got to do is to pick out your bad bottle-necks and start scraping 'em when it starts snowing. Stop your traffic every once in a while and scrape it clear. Have a good cache of sand there and keep the surface well strewn. Then your traffic will keep moving and no jam will build up. Why, he added with a wave of the hand, the people who have your streets in charge ought to pick out some bright young chap and send him up to some good-sized New England town—

any one, Haverhill, Worcester, Springfield, it doesn't matter —for a month or so in the dead of winter. With a couple of good snowstorms he could learn all the tricks of the trade. And believe me, brother, it's quite a trick too, this keeping your town functioning through a bad fall of snow.

After the first snow has come and has gone and the threatened cold fronts merge to form the usual winter weather, the birds commence to cluster around the house, handy to their feeding stations. These have been carefully located, not with any thought of their convenience, but to occupy a vantage point that can be reconnoitered from a window.

Thus from the lowest limb of the white oak that stands next the west kitchen window there hangs, just above the level of the eye, an old black coconut shell well packed with white suet. Outside the other window, in the thick rhododendrons, there is another suet holder; and through the tangle of black limb and green leaves there can be glimpsed the hanging tin contraption—a holder for the sunflower seeds, ground-up peanuts, and all the bits of grain that go to make up birdseed. Finally, within easy reach of a limb of the dogwood standing by the well between the kitchen and the woodshed there is a curious rig—a small log honeycombed with auger holes that are kept packed with peanut butter.

This last is the rendezvous of a pair of white-breasted nuthatches. First, I see one in the branches of the dogwood, running skillfully along and around a branch and giving it a thorough going over with his bill that seems so long in proportion to the rest of his chunkiness. That black cap of his will cause the unwary to mistake him for the familiar chickadee. But the *dee-dee-dee* is missing. Instead there is a small wiry twitter and a short *gnah gnah gnah* repeated three or four times between twitters. A smartly caparisoned little thing he is, with a slate-blue back and tail feathers slashed with black and white against the blue. This is ever in sharp contrast with his pure white breast that fits up and almost around his neck like a choker.

Wait now! He has flown to the top of the peanut butter stick. Down he goes head first, stopping to bury that long bill in the soft brown peanut butter. *Gnah gnah gnah.* His companion in the dogwood is busily circumnavigating the trunk and he likewise is descending upside down.

Day after day now I can count on these birds stabbing upside down at the suet of the coconut or traveling head down on the peanut butter stick, the air alive with their little twitter and the *gnah gnah gnah.* Very friendly they are and they do not fly until I am nearly at arm's length, and then only up into the dogwood, to return to their feast so soon as I am on my way to the woodshed for an armful of firewood. *Gnah gnah gnah.* Upside-down birds, I call them.

Late in a winter afternoon with the sun slanting through the trees and their branches standing each one in the clarity of some magical tracery against the sky, and when the snow shines with that blue light peculiar to it in the woods—that is the time to be out there with your tools and get a head start on next winter's wood. For then comes the solid satisfaction to be had as the axe, biting deep into the log, marks off one edge of the chip which, with the next cut, will spin far out into the snow. You know a woodsman by the size of his chips —so the saying goes up there along the Penobscot north of Bangor.

There is a set of tools that goes with this. Out in the woodshed sunk in the chopping block at a graspable angle is the axe. That maple handle is hand made, turned out with a crooked knife by an old woodsman. Hard by stands a sledge, all eight pounds of it, and beside it a couple of battered wedges. Then stretching along the wall there on wooden pegs is the double-ended saw and below it a bucksaw. These are the tools of this trade.

And there is oak, maple, beech, hickory, and sycamore towering aloft out of the thick underbrush in Bringhurst Woods. I only take the dead ones and the windfalls, and that is plenty of wood and plenty of work.

The exercise to be had out there on one end of that double-ended saw is rugged. Back and forth two backs rise and fall in an easy rolling rhythm as the saw rasps, biting deeper and deeper with each cut into a long log of white oak. Your breath comes quicker and—you note with relief—so does that of your companion. Then all of a sudden the saw binds. She will not budge. A couple of taps on a wedge inserted in the cut cures this, and then in jig time the saw cuts through, tearing down into the leaf mold. With sledge and wedge and axe the log now splits quickly into four quarters. Then the bucksaw takes over. And after a bit a series of square wood-piles betrays the line of your work.

Well do I remember late one winter afternoon when the sun's rays were slanting eastward through the trees. The air was growing sharp and the melting snow had begun to freeze. In subtle response to this rhythm of nature, the *chunk* of my axe began to increase its tempo. With one swing a wedge-shaped chip took form. With the next swing into the opposite kerf, the chip spun out into the snow. *Chunk— chunk—chunk*—the cut went deep, well past the heart. Then came a back-handed swing. Well aimed, it sliced up through the back of the cut, and the log fell free.

The sun was gone. To the westward the trunks and the limbs of the trees stood fretted against a bank of deep red. Overhead the afterglow was forming and the underbellies of the small clouds were beginning to glow with pink. Motionless the trees stood like set pieces, each limb a sharp line in this colored atmosphere. It was chill. Again the chopping commenced. *Chunk—chunk—chunk.*

Then from afar there came an alien yet familiar noise. *Aaah—oogh*—the single broken call of a wild goose. The steady chopping continued. *Chunk—chunk—chunk.*

Now they are straight overhead, just clear of the treetops —eight of them, their long necks outstretched, on silently wavering wings. The gander sees me and the aisles of the wood ring with his wild cries. They flare. In that instant the afterglow tinges their long white breasts with pink. Then they are gone—gabbling, honking, calling.

Afterward I wondered. Was it the *chunk* of my axe that had brought them in so straight overhead? Probably.

The end of such a winter day oftentimes comes with startling abruptness when a man is out splitting and stacking next winter's supply. Rhythmically and evenly the axe rises and falls, and with each swing a stout square chunk of red oak splits clean and true. With the log now split eight-wise on the snow, I sink my axe in the next butt and leaning over, start my stacking. The square crib rises and when the last stick is in place, I stop and straighten up for a breather.

Then of a sudden I am aware of the change. Twilight and dusk have crept upon me unaware. The snow is no longer white. It is gray. Above the fretted branches the sky has lost its blue to a steel gray. Only in the west is there color. Unnoticed the sun has sunk and there beyond the interlacing bare branches and trunks of the trees, an effulgence of cold crimson is fading swiftly as if reflecting the dying embers of some vast conflagration. As I watch the western sky, a deeper shade of red emerges that grows darker and darker until shortly it will merge with the darkness. Already deep shadows have fallen in the woods.

I stir. Time to pick up the wedges, to shoulder the sledge and axe, and to head for home where that hot supper awaits —tea, a gleaming golden johnnycake, and a goodly mess of steaming baked beans.

And at night when the blasts of a no'the-easter are whistling around the corners of the house, there is more solid satisfaction to be had when I toss a chunk of that wood— fashioned with my own tool and hand—on top of the fire. A shower of sparks leaps aloft, and the flames lick their way around the clean split edges of the stick. There is real ease for you.

There is that round back-log of dogwood that burns so slowly and so steadily that it will, toward the end of the evening, consume itself to a white powdery ash. It touches memories. It has its history. Well do I remember in spring after spring of the year the white beauty of those three dogwoods, now cut and piled, and their ghostly appearance in the woods in the moonlight of early May. Many a time I trimmed them as they slowly lost their last strength; and then at last came the felling, the sawing into lengths, and the careful piling crib-fashion so that they would dry through and through.

And there is that billet of white oak that burns in front. A victim of Hurricane Hazel this—a fine tall oak that came crashing to earth, felled by the turbulent fury of the blow. I recall the woodsmen who came here to snake out the blowdowns and haul them off to a Jersey sawmill—a slender young fellow who performed miracles of maneuver with what he called a cat—a caterpillar tractor—and his partner, a great broad-beamed colored man with a voice that seemed to come out of a gravel pit and a good-natured grin as broad as his beam. They cut off the butt of the stump of this white oak, and left it for me to split.

And split it I did with sledge, wedge, and axe, and now as it burns and warms me for the second time, I sense again the peculiar satisfaction that derived from the task—how it split so fair and clean, and how it stacked so neat and square.

These two—dogwood and white oak—make fit companions for a good open fire of a cold winter evening with the wind on the prowl outside.

A winter thunderstorm is a rare phenomenon, and its aftermath on this occasion was still more rare. The clearing came suddenly at sundown and the heavy louring clouds were like a canopy hung in the heavens. Over in the southeast quarter an eyebrow was lifting—the sure sign of a shift in the wind. Then with startling rapidity the dramatic scene unfolded before my eyes. Rarely do the eastern and the western horizons present so vast, so elemental a contrast.

In the west a winter sunset lined the sky with alternate bands of black cloud and red sky. Then in the opposite quarter beyond the bare limbs of the trees there towered high into the heavens great round masses of cumulus. Vast and elemental they were and of pure gleaming white, as white as driven snow. At the edges of these rounding and gleaming white bulges the sky was of the deep dark blue of evening, stabbed here and there with a glint of yellow—a star.

Then of a sudden the whole dramatic spectacle was illumined with a baleful glare as silent lightning flared amid and lit up the vast rounded contours of these cumuli. It was as if somewhere there in back of that great white cloud bank, Vulcan was at work at his anvil forging thunderbolts for the passing storm. It was awesome—and terrifyingly beautiful.

I fully expected Jupiter to arise full-bearded above those white clouds, to hurl down his thunderbolt, and roar forth to an awe-struck world:

"Ecce cumuli, homines."

But of all the sights of winter, incomparably the most exciting and the most beautiful is the ice storm. On the early March day of which I write, Bringhurst Woods had been encased in ice. Upon awakening I could see that the branches of the beech just outside the window were sheathed with it. The red of the budding of the maple outside another window shone through its lustre. Out in back the dogwood was a miracle of gray crystal. No breath of air was stirring, and the trees stood in frigid silence. In looking out across the open field toward the line of oaks at the edge of the ridge, I was struck by the shades of grayness. First there were the frozen stalks of the weeds and grass, all grayness in the field, then the trees, each twig swollen to twice its size, another shade of gray, and beyond the dull darkening gray of the sky.

It remained thus until the late forenoon, and then snow commenced to fall in large silent flakes that at first were melting upon touching the moist earth. The trees soon accumulated an extra overcoating of snow on top of the ice, thus enhancing the shades of gray. All day long this boreal scene was gray. There was no sign of the sun. There was no wind. This was unusual, for ordinarily the climax of an ice storm is both wind and sun, and its beauty is so evanescent that I take myself to task for not observing it constantly.

In the late afternoon I took a long walk to observe familiar scenes garbed in such unusual beauty. A holly tree was a rare sight—snow-crowned, with small icicles pendent from the sharp points of its green leaves. Amid the frozen foliage, the round berries gleamed rich in their redness, heightened by the moisture, at once frozen and melting. Amid all this snow and ice there were thrusting up out of the dark moist leaf mold at the foot of a tall spruce the gleaming green leaves of a clump of snowdrops. And the tender tips of daffodils and tulips were also piercing the melting snow.

I fixed my glasses on the Norway spruce. In its top it is a dead tree, and its aspect was in marked contrast to the lower branches where the snow hung heavy, piled on the matted green needles. A white pine that towered above a stretch of sprout land presented in the round field of the glass a tortured aspect of frozen stillness. At a distance where I saw the woods as the skyline, it was as if I were looking at a forest of gray crystal.

I turned into the woods to make my way down to Turkey Run, brushing aside as I passed the ice-laden branches and tops of the small trees bent across my path. The stream was full and yellow in color contrasting strangely with this ice-gray world. Where at a bend in the stream a dam has flowed out a small pool, a great dead stub of an ancient oak towers aloft. Its blackness was enhanced by its skin of ice. Following on down the course of the run, I came to the foot of the ridge where the stream suddenly ceases tumbling, and I heard a chorus of alarmed quacking. But the snow-laden brush was so thick that I could not see from whence this came. Later, when I came out on the highway I looked back to see six duck swimming swiftly on the surface of the small dammed-up pool. There were two mallard drakes and four hens. The iridescent sheen of green on the heads and purple on the wings were the only spots of color in all this gray world of ice and snow.

Following along the highway at almost every step there were little crashes of ice falling on the concrete or bouncing off the tops of passing cars. I soon left the highway and started up the long curve of graveled road that leads up over the ridge of rocks from whence the Bringhurst estate derives its name of Rockwood. Here tall and stately hemlocks in scattered array were garbed in white patterns of snow, their contrast with the stark ice-laden limbs of the hardwood growth never more marked. Upon reaching the crest I came suddenly upon a dogwood, a spreading dome of delicate crystal tracery.

At this moment the gray clouds were parting. At first their ashen hue was lit with a roseate glow. I raised my glasses and watched the slow descent of the sun—a great orb of orange-red seen dimly through the clouds that were rising and drifting across it in long gray wisps. The effect was of a great hole slowly burning in a gray blanket. Aloft, high in the sky, I saw that it was clearing. The sky there was now blue and this made me mindful of the morrow. For if it should come off cold, as it now threatened to do, and if no wind should arise, I would have the rare privilege of watching this arctic scene in the light of the morning sun.

The sun soon dropped from sight behind the low-lying cloud bank and the upper sky was suffused with faint shades of light, so faint that they were not colors. They only suggested them and served to enhance the existing effects—the limbs black in their encasement of ice, the variant shades of gray that existed in the vistas where the trees shouldered against the ashen sky and above in the eastern quarter where the bold line of the cloud bank lay furled against the horizon.

That night the stars bespoke a clear day to come. The cold hung on and no wind blew, and in consequence the early morning sun shot glancing rays off an ice-crystal world.

Fortified only by a cup of tea, I was up and abroad early. The ice was shattering from the trees and the woods resounded with a steady rasping that was the combination of a myriad minute crashings. I picked up a piece of this fallen ice. The enclasping curve around the branch was still there and, at its thickest, it was at least a quarter of an inch thick.

I walked in the walled rose garden where the rays of the early sun had not yet reached. There the lawn, the orderly boxwood, and the rose arbors were still white with the snow and ice of the day before. From this vantage the tops of Bringhurst Woods are visible in three of the four quarters and I lifted my glasses to them. Each type of tree was its own crystal chandelier. The beeches made a particularly lovely showing, their tops presenting great bending sheafs of iced branches sparkling in the early sunlight. The oaks, less delicate, stood in contrast, holding in a frigid fixity each small finger of a twig. The tulip poplars towered in stately magnificence, their trunks shining black beneath the ice.

As I stood in the snow-covered rose garden watching the glinting and the glancing of the sunlight off this crystallized foliage, a slight breeze touched the tops of the trees. Then they swung to and fro in a stately manner and with a cold dignity as showers of shattered ice fell to the ground. At this moment two crows were to be seen winging and cawing across the sky above the wintry landscape.

I moved out of the garden and past the big house to the edge of the ridge from whence I could look out over the descending sprout land to the tall woods beyond. No habitation was in sight, only this vista of ice-encased foliage and trees. This was fairyland. The sun was now out in full force and all the world was asparkle. High in the sky a brace of wildfowl swinging on set wings looked for a pool free of ice. Failing to find it, they lined out for the river. Then I lost them to sight. I heard a jay scream its harsh note. Turning my back to the sun and the scene, I observed that the straight trunk of the tulip poplar beneath which I was standing was black with water running down the ridges of the bark. At its base a slight cloud of steam was rising from the dank leaf mold.

The songbirds again became a part of life. The afternoon before I had seen but two—a single junco, and a startled robin that took refuge in the thick branches of a hemlock. Now I heard a cardinal's call of *What cheer* from a thicket of rhododendron, the crows cawing and flying, the scream of a jay, and a Carolina wren making the world ring with liquid callings.

All the while this fragile world of crystal beauty was disintegrating before my eyes. For a bit there was a seeming respite, though the melting continued even when the sun climbed up behind a cloud. Soon it was out again, and as these notes were written, the trees became but the shadow of the height of their frozen glory.

This ice storm was one for long remembering.

Rich are those who respond to the ever-present rhythm of nature in the cycle of the seasons. Here it is but the start of March, yet the harbingers of spring are already at hand. Of this a turn around Bringhurst Woods is a sufficient evidence.

Overhead the tracery of bare branches weaves back and forth against the now scudding overcast and again the blue open sky. At these latter moments the sun comes through and warms my back despite a wind that is still finger cold.

Underfoot the ground is springy with the deep moisture gurgling beneath the thin covering of dried brown leaves. Ahead lies a patch of dull green. It is myrtle caught and still clasped by the grip of winter's cold. But in the middle there, what is that?

The brown leaves are slightly uplifted and I kneel to investigate. Then I pull the sere leaves aside and there they are—tender green shoots yellowing at their base and rising into clear live green where here and there they have pierced the leaf mold that has imprisoned them. Small nodules—the buds—are forming and there just ahead is the hardiest of all. Delicately bent, a flower nods toward the earth, its gleaming white petals hiding the pale green inner heart of the blossom.

What is it? The first snowdrop!

This is Nature's sign manual. Winter is on the wane. The hidden sap is running. Soon now the maples will be blushing, the blossoms will be spotting the grass, and the birds migrating. The eternal cycle of the seasons has run its course, and once again the spring of the year is at hand.

In Retrospect

The why and the wherefore of this book call for statement. This is a parlous undertaking. It involves a long journey back over the years into the forming of my mind in its endless interaction with environment. Moreover the tracking of the origin of any idea to its source is a matter of great dubiety. Ordinarily the event is inexplicable—an inbursting of the mind—a miracle that comes to be. Occasionally a contemporary record will provide the clue. But this is rare. And generally in retrospect the mind seizes upon some occurrence that may have played its small part in genesis or parturition. Thus:

Years ago at a now long since abandoned depot on the Boston and Maine where the tracks trend eastward in a long traverse of a wide salt marsh, there was an old Yankee in charge by the name of Fred Walker. In the spring of the year and in the fall of the year it was his custom to take note of the small events of field and marsh and make a record of them. His mode of recording was odd. Each spring he would get himself a long slab of white pine and plane it down smooth. On this he would scrawl at the top with his stub of a pencil, the year—1900, let us say.

Then there would follow the laconic entries of the unfolding of the spring of the year—the day when the first geese went over, the day he saw his first bluebird, when he heard the whistle of yellowleg out over the marsh, saw the first dandelion and buttercup spotting the grass on the far side of the tracks. Then about midlength of the white pine slab, he would mark off a division line. Below this would come his depiction of the fall of the year—the morning that the swamp maple at the edge of Leavitt's woodlot turned to crimson against the green, when the black duck began to fly in, the day he saw a buck crossing the tracks, when the pa'tridge scattered, and later in the season his record of the first sugaring of snow and when the glass first stood at zero.

Come the end of the year old Fred would take his slab and nail it up on the side of the depot in the shelter of the eave alongside last year's slab so that folks, when they were standing around on the platform waiting for the old wheezing local to come to a stop to let them aboard and lug them in to Portland, could see how matters stood on that day the year before, or five years previous, perchance.

Then one day old Fred died. There was some talk of taking his old slabs and lugging them in to the local Society of Natural History. But it was only talk. Nobody ever did anything about it. Then after a while the railroad quit running passenger trains that would stop there, and the fellow that succeeded Fred had nothing to do but handle freight. The next thing you knew the trucks took to hauling the clams and lobsters out of there and even the freights did not stop any more. So they boarded up the doors and windows of the old depot and the only sign of life around it was the line of fat white gulls that would set on the ridge of the roof on sunny days.

Today, about this old abandoned depot the fish hawk screams as he circles over the marshes, the beetleheads fly uttering their appealing whistles, and the white-throated sparrow sings to burst his heart in the spring of the year, but no one makes a record of these important events. Still, if you go there, they tell me you can still decipher the weather-beaten records of old Fred Walker of how it was at the Pine Point depot in the spring and in the fall of the year half a century ago.

At the time of these recordings I was a little barefoot shaver, but I used to read them and they made their impression.

Then early in the game, albeit precisely when I cannot now tell, there grew the habit of what I choose to term the indulgence of moods. These would come into being in the course of some commonplace experience—a midwinter walk at midnight beneath a black vault studded with stabs of light with the frozen surface of the roadway crackling aloud with every step—listening to the low moaning of a distant foghorn muted by the falling of silently slanting snow—the feeling of companionable loneliness that is the gift of fog and that used to impel me to shove off in a single scull and lose my bearings. Then I would rest on my oars and listen to the tuneless tolling of a hidden bell buoy, the rushing of the passing wake of some unseen craft, and the disembodied sounds from up ashore—the barking of a dog, the gabble of children, the nicker of a horse.

Each of these small events gave rise to its own mood in which the exultation of physical enjoyment was and is the essence of the experience. I found that I could repeat these varied experiences and thus re-create and indulge again their moods. In this manner the interaction of environment, event, and my own sensory apparatus wove and rewove and to this day weaves and reweaves the texture of my experience.

There comes to mind another experience of incalculable generative influence in the making of this book. The scene is a college classroom. I well remember a certain professor as he stood one day in the spring of 1917 by his blackboard, sparse, angular and nervously alert. On it while muttering some sort of incantation, he had scrawled in utterly incomprehensible hieroglyphics his six terse and forceful maxims for good writing. And there was I asking him what in the devil they were, and why in the hell he did not write them so they could be read. Came the quizzical glance so characteristic of the man and then:

"Ah! That is the point, you see. The really curious come down and ask me. And then they do not forget."

The incident led to long hours of companionship while we talked the moon down the sky. His has been an immeasurable influence, and it is altogether fitting and proper that I should here pay tribute to the creative genius of the late John M. Berdan.

In the summer and fall of 1921 I made a memorable excursion—in the parlance of the Maine woods—a river trip. Ascending by canoe to the headwaters of the Penobscot and then, after a portage across the height o' land into St. John Pond, descending the St. John, in the first month we traversed the Maine woods. In the second month going up the Tobique and down the Nepisiguit, we crossed the Province of New Brunswick—"de longes' reever treep ever was take out o' de town o' Greenville." Such was the claim of my French-Canadian guide.

In a sense this book then got its start. For the taking of the square-tail trout in Sordy-hunk, the episode of the crows lost in the fog, the death of the crane in the cove, and the spoliation of the red leaves of the swamp maple by the first spitting of snow—all these occurred and are of record of that time. In other years there have been other river trips and of all of them I have countless notes and recorded impressions. Then within the past decade I have been recording my experiences, new and old, for publication.

What has been here presented has a twofold aspect. In the first place my aim at all times is to keep myself alert and attuned to the end that whatever takes place in my small segment of the sphere is received into my consciousness at its fullest impact. Thereby I acquire experiences worth owning. The other aspect of the business is this. It is to render a faithful accounting of the event, so faithful as to evoke again the mood evoked by the experience. To the extent that this is achieved, I have been successful; in the degree that the result falls short of this goal, there is failure.

To the experiences that I have recounted I could add instances without number. Sometimes they occur with the sudden effect of an apparition as when, while driving on some commonplace errand, there flashed in swift flight across the road out of the trees on one side and into the trees on the other, a small hawk. In front of the car it flared, and in that instant of flight I saw clutched in its talons the gray body of a luckless field mouse.

Other times there are signals as when walking in the bare woods in early spring, shadows flashing down the trunks of trees and across the forest floor tell of the wide circling of wide-winged buzzards.

The event may be dramatic. I recall one April morning when the trees were shrouded with gray mist, that a pair of wild geese chose the orchard for their mating. What an alarum and excursion! Both sight and sound were startling— now and again the great powerful bodies zooming around just over the tops of the blossoming apple trees, filling the air for an hour and more with their raucous outcries and plaintive honkings.

But it is by no means all happenchance. I know where in Bringhurst Woods the purple periwinkle spreads its green carpet in the widest expanse, where the day lilies will come on to bloom in an orange profusion, and where along the brook in late summer the cardinal flowers will stand like scarlet sentinels. On these and on many another spot I keep a watchful eye. And I can anticipate the midwinter night when I shall be setting fire to the slash pile that I may watch on the white snow the ruddy reflection of the flames and the shadows that will waver in the long aisles of the woods.

Again I may make small excursions to well remembered places—to the hidden willow swale where red-wing black-birds swing on swaying reeds, where bobwhite call *bob white* from ridge to ridge and where this spring I watched for half an hour outlined against a pearl-gray tent cater-pillar's triangular nest the startling bit of flaming orange and black that is the golden robin—a Baltimore oriole feasting on the imprisoned grubs.

Then I may wend my way down to Thousand Acre Marsh in order once again to sniff the fresh scent of the marsh and thereby enjoy one of those fleeting moments when retrospect and anticipation are merged in an equal savor. And, as I did upon that recent visit there, I will return with a picture graved in my mind—this time of a duck swimming in a dis-tant cut leaving a widening wake, the whole small scene etched in lines of gold. This extraordinary effect had caught my eye at the precise moment and at the exact angle for its reflected creation by the slanting rays of the falling sun.

Perhaps it is the simplest event that is the most memorable, like the rain that came unexpected on a recent night. As I lay in the still dark air, sleepless and waiting for sleep to come, the sporadic spatter of the early drops came faintly to ear. They were scattered taps. They followed no rhythm and they played no tune. In my mind's eye I could see in the aisles of the darkened woods a leaf here and a leaf there in a beech or an oak and now in some tall tulip poplar, suddenly depressed. It was as if they were the keys of some great natural instrument being hit by the invisible fingers of an invisible player.

The desultory tapping continued for a while. It was prelude to the play and its crescendo was a slow and gentle thing. Now and again the suggestion of wind, a mere breath of moving air, supplied a background of faint rustling for the tapping, as it fluttered the leaves in its passing. Then the wind, that was later to be, died aborning, and again there was but the darkness and the intermittent but relentless tapping of the drops on the invisible leaves.

At some stage, yet so subtly, so slowly, and so softly as to render it impossible for me to pin the precise moment of the change, the frequency of this irregular tapping began to multiply. Finally it merged in a distinct and different theme. This was the second movement of the symphony of the rain. This movement was quite another thing. The merging of the pattering had given rise to a steady noise like the remote rolling of a myriad small drums. No longer was it theme, it was chorus against which new small noises of the downpouring rain supplied new themes.

As the gutters filled there sounded in the downspouts the throaty gurgle that was the voice of pouring water. In the dry leaves sheltered by the rhododendrons outside the open window the splatter was in a higher key. The drumming tattoo on the shingles just over my head, that too stood forth against the steady downpouring of the fast-falling rain. And subtly in the background there was the trickle of running water and the sucking sound of seepage down into the softened soil.

Suddenly in response to the summons of the invisible baton there came the crescendo, a swelling volume as a cat's-paw of wind struck the leaves of the beech, the oaks, and the poplars with a sudden swish. Then it mounted in strength, fortissimo, as the cat's-paw grew to a gust. For the moment of its passage all the varied notes of the falling rain stood forth in the intensity of contrast, heightened by the swishing and thrashing of the sodden leaves.

My mind drifted with the rise and fall of this symphony of the rain. I remembered other rains on other nights on other roofs. I recalled the roaring of the wind when a no'the-easter blows, saw again the sharp sweep of rain-laden leaves against wet panes, listened for the sharp slap of hard-falling rain on hard pavements, felt the shaking of the timbers and heard their creaking as the blasts of the storm shook the house. Then in this drifting dream I fell asleep, to sleep for I know not how long.

When I awoke—and this was the cause of my awakening —the rain had ceased. And in the final movement of this natural symphony there was a return to the first movement of the rain—a gentle, irregular, and desultory tapping that came, this time, however, from the dripping from the rain-laden leaves.

This is the way of my life. It has been so over the years. It will be so, God willing, to the end and the beginning of the long excursion that will have no end.

Acknowledgment

Some of the material in this book has appeared in different form in the columns of the *Wilmington Morning News* and the *Journal-Every Evening*, both of Wilmington, Delaware, and a part of the description of the no'the-east storm on pages 85-88 in the *Christian Science Monitor*, and they are here presented with the permission of the editors to whom acknowledgment is justly due and is hereby made.